WINE BAR FOOD

WINE BAR FOOD

MEDITERRANEAN FLAVORS TO CRAVE WITH WINES TO MATCH

CATHY AND TONY MANTUANO

PHOTOGRAPHS BY JEFF KAUCK

CLARKSON POTTER PUBLISHERS
NEW YORK

TO CARLO

Copyright © 2008 by Cathy Mantuano
and Tony Mantuano
Photographs copyright © 2008 byJeff Kauck

Published in the United States by Clarkson Potter/Publishers,
an imprint of the Crown Publishing Group,
a division of Random House, Inc., New York.
www.crownpublishing.com
www.clarksonpotter.com

Clarkson N. Potter is a trademark
and Potter and colophon
are registered trademarks of
Random House, Inc.

Library of Congress Cataloging-in-Publication Data
Mantuano, Cathy, 1958–
    Wine bar food : Mediterranean flavors to crave
    with wines to match / by Cathy and Tony Mantuano;
    photographs by Jeff Kauck. — 1st ed.
    Includes index.
1. Appetizers—Mediterranean Region.
2. Snack foods—Mediterranean Region.
3. Cookery, Mediterranean.
4. Wine and wine making—Mediterranean Region.
    I. Mantuano, Tony, 1954- II. Title
TX740.M2575   2008
641.591822—dc22   2007043010

ISBN 978-0-307-35279-8

Printed in China

Design by MAGGIE HINDERS

10 9 8 7 6 5 4

First Edition

CONTENTS

INTRODUCTION

FROM TAPAS IN SEVILLE TO CICHETTI IN VENICE, the cities of the Mediterranean have a long history of wine bars, places to gather and discuss the events of the day while enjoying some Treviso Marmalade and Goat Cheese Crostini with a glass of sparkling wine or some prosciutto and salami with a fruity bottle of Barbera. The custom to simply unwind with a bite of something incredible and a sip of wine after work replenishes the soul. Big decisions such as what is for dinner can wait—indefinitely in fact; patrons often make a meal of these irresistible small plates, hopping from bar to bar to try the house specialty and meet up with new groups of friends.

Some European wine bars are traditional in atmosphere, decorated with large wine barrels and dusty old bottles. But nowadays, especially in larger cities, there are wine bars with sleek counters and high-tech lighting serving prized local ingredients in new and exciting modern dishes such as Falafel Crab Cakes or Yellowtail Carpaccio with Citrus and Fennel.

Americans have adopted the a-little-bit-of-this-and-a-sip-of-that mentality wholeheartedly. Wine bars are popping up all over the United States, and not just in major cities. While we love the elegance and precision of our high-end restaurant in Chicago, Spiaggia, we longed for a convivial gathering spot of our own, someplace where we could serve tasting portions of food to share, encourage guests to eat with their fingers, and re-create the wonderful experiences we've had living in Italy and traveling across Europe. Our new wine bar, Enoteca Spiaggia, in Miami's South Beach district, will be where we do just that. Designed by Todd Oldham, this high-style wine bar is the realization of all the things we love about wine bars, and serves many of the recipes from this book. (The warm, Mediterranean-like climate of southern Florida doesn't hurt either!)

Throughout our careers running restaurants, our greatest satisfaction has come from pleasing our guests. Creating flavorful menus and pairing them with great wine is our work and our passion. It's easy to see why what people want now is easy-to-serve dishes that deliver big, fresh flavors with minimal effort, the dishes that make wine bars across the globe dining destinations.

Wine bar food is unpretentious and straightforward, relying on quality ingredients, simply prepared. Many of these recipes can be made in advance and presented warm, at room temperature, or chilled and are as perfect for weeknight meals as they are for entertaining. The dishes can be served in true wine bar spirit as small plates to be shared by many, with everyone getting little tastes of lots of dishes, but they can also be served to a smaller group in more traditional appetizer and main-course servings. Where applicable, we've noted in the recipes how many tasting, appetizer, main-course, or side-dish portions a dish makes.

This book is a culmination of years of traveling and eating across the Mediterranean. Our inspiration has come from enjoying Manzanilla sherry with locally caught fried fish on the coast of Spain in Sanlúcar, where Columbus set sail, or dining on Steak Tagliata with Arugula and a great bottle of Chianti Classico with friends in Tuscany. In *Wine Bar Food*, we have compiled some of our best food and wine experiences for you to reproduce and enjoy in your own home.

Each chapter in this book evokes the wine bar style of a particular European city, with recipes and wines inspired by the region. Though our travels have taken us off the beaten path, each recipe in this book has been carefully crafted with the American home cook in mind, using ingredients familiar on these shores. We have included a Resource Guide for specialty ingredients that we think are just too good for you to miss. The wines we recommend are affordable and can be found on this side of the Atlantic.

And while these recipes may interpret traditional dishes, many treat classic flavors with a modern twist. You should feel free to mix recipes from different cities to create a meal. The point is to bring a little bit of the wine bar lifestyle into your home. It's all about respecting good food, good wine, and simple technique in enjoying the food and wine of our modern world. To us, this fun and approachable attitude is one of the most attractive aspects of the wine bar.

We have also included three special sections on foods that can easily make a no-cook meal, important components of wine bar food. One explains the dazzling variety of delicious cured meats now available in this country. Another explores imported cheeses—ones that are easily found in the United States and shouldn't be missed. Both include instructions for serving these crowd-pleasing foods that require hardly any preparation.

A final section shares our favorite time-saving, high-quality imported tinned and bottled products that are now available to home cooks. What was once a culinary taboo—store-bought, not homemade!—is actually an authentic and smart way to create a meal. These exciting foods will make your life easier without sacrificing taste.

The commonsense approach to pairing food and wine holds that wines of the region always go with the food of a region. We couldn't agree more. To that end, within each chapter we explore the wines of the area at hand and pick our favorites, keeping in mind what is available in the United States. We hope you'll find some new wines to try among these gems.

While the focus is primarily on wine as the drink to accompany these recipes, we would be remiss not to offer some of the wonderful, unique cocktails that we have encountered over the years. Some are wine based, but all of them are fun and festive, adding another dimension to any party and pairing well with the dishes of their region.

The crucial elements in wine-bar food are simplicity and quality. Start with something irresistible and add a glass of wine—or the other way around. Whatever you do, don't overthink it. Serve terrific ingredients and satisfying wines and your home will be as warm and welcoming as anywhere on the Mediterranean.

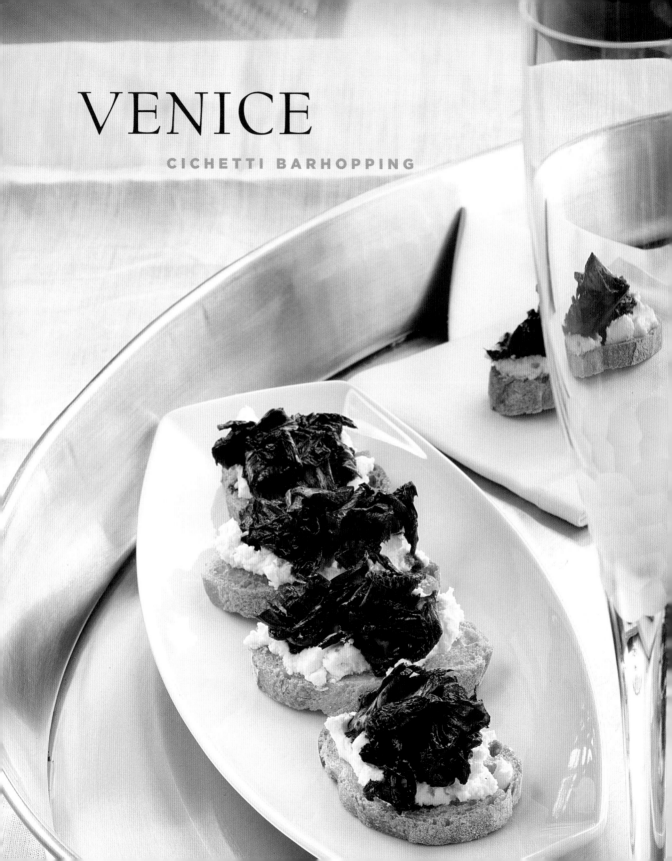

VENICE

CICHETTI BARHOPPING

CICHETTI are the small tastes of food that accompany a glass of wine or a cocktail in the neighborhood wine bar, the Venetian *bacari.* Here we have created cichetti of our own, inspired by long evenings strolling through the residential *sestieri* (or districts of Venice), discovering small wine bars along the way. Offering festive sparkling wine-based cocktails, modern seafood dishes, traditional Venetian sandwiches called *tramezzini,* and more, this chapter transports you to the ancient city of 160 canals.

Bellini Cocktail

Rossini Cocktail

Tiziano Cocktail

Marinated Olives

Treviso Marmalade and Goat Cheese Crostini

Lemony Shrimp with Currants and Pine Nuts

Whipped Baccalà with Polenta Crostini

Grilled Chicken and Roasted Tomato on Semolina Bread

Shrimp, Arugula, and Caper Mayonnaise on Brioche

Sautéed Mushrooms and Sweet Garlic with White Polenta

Black Pasta with Scungilli and Tomato

Amaretto Polenta Pound Cake

The Wines of the Veneto, Friuli–Venezia Giulia, and Trentino–Alto Adige

BELLINI COCKTAIL

BELLINI COCKTAIL This sparkling wine drink, invented at the famous Harry's Bar in Venice, is made there with white peach juice, though yellow peach juice would also be delicious. Serve this at brunch or at cocktail hour, especially in summer. • MAKES 1 COCKTAIL

In a champagne flute, combine the juice and the wine.

2 ounces chilled peach juice or peach nectar

4 ounces chilled Prosecco or other dry sparkling wine

ROSSINI COCKTAIL

To make this fruity sparkling wine drink, substitute strawberry juice for the peach juice.

TIZIANO COCKTAIL

Perfect for fall, this refreshing cocktail substitutes Concord grape juice for the peach juice.

MARINATED OLIVES

MARINATED OLIVES Large and meaty, Cerignola olives are either black or bright green, depending on maturity. For marinating, we prefer the firmer-textured supercolossal green olives. The orange zest highlights the olives' inherent sweetness while adding a splash of color. • MAKES 3 CUPS

In a large bowl, combine the olives with the olive oil, garlic, orange zest, orange juice, and fennel seeds. Cover and marinate in the refrigerator overnight or for up to 5 days. Bring the olives to room temperature before serving.

Stir the olives and transfer to a small dish to serve.

3 cups Cerignola olives

2 tablespoons olive oil

2 garlic cloves, finely chopped

Zest of 1 orange, removed in strips with a vegetable peeler

$^2/_3$ cup fresh orange juice

1 tablespoon fennel seeds, toasted and coarsely ground

TREVISO MARMALADE AND GOAT CHEESE CROSTINI

Creamy, sweet, crunchy, and tart all in one bite, these colorful crostini pair nicely with a glass of Valpolicella or other fruity red wine. Treviso is the long purplish lettuce that looks like Belgian endive but is actually part of the radicchio family. Filone is the Italian equivalent of a baguette. If you can find it, by all means use it here. See photograph on page x. • **MAKES 16 CROSTINI**

2 heads of treviso or Belgian endive

2 tablespoons extra virgin olive oil

1/2 cup balsamic vinegar

2 tablespoons sugar

Sixteen 1/4-inch-thick slices filone or baguette

6 ounces fresh goat cheese, softened to room temperature

Trim 1/2 inch off the bottom of the treviso and discard. Halve the treviso lengthwise, cut out the hard inner core, and coarsely chop the leaves.

Heat the olive oil in a medium saucepan over medium heat. Add the treviso and cook until wilted, stirring frequently, 7 to 8 minutes. Stir in the vinegar and sugar, reduce the heat to medium-low, and continue cooking until the mixture is reduced to a jamlike consistency, 20 to 25 minutes. Set aside to cool.

Preheat the broiler.

To make the crostini, lay out the slices of bread on a cookie sheet. Toast under the broiler until brown, about 1 minute. Flip the slices over and repeat. Remove from the oven and set aside.

Spread a thick layer of goat cheese onto each crostino. Top with some treviso marmalade and serve at room temperature.

LEMONY SHRIMP WITH CURRANTS AND PINE NUTS

A traditional Venetian dish, this combination of puckery, sweet, and nutty flavors is paired with fresh sardines or other small fish, though we love it with shrimp. A hot marinade barely cooks the shrimp, leaving them tender and succulent. Enjoy them with another Venetian classic, a glass of Prosecco. • **SERVES 4 TO 6 AS AN APPETIZER**

Soak the currants in the vinegar for 10 minutes, then drain and set aside. Put the shrimp in a glass baking dish large enough to hold them snugly.

Heat the olive oil in a medium saucepan over medium heat. Add the shallot and cook until soft, 4 to 5 minutes. Stir in the lemon juice, sugar, salt, and pepper and continue cooking for 1 minute, until well blended.

Pour the hot marinade over the shrimp. Add the currants and pine nuts and stir the mixture to combine.

Refrigerate for at least 3 hours or up to 2 days, stirring the shrimp once or twice. Remove from the refrigerator and let sit at room temperature for 30 minutes before serving.

To serve, arrange the shrimp on a platter, scattering the currants and pine nuts on top and drizzling with the marinade.

$1/4$ cup currants or raisins

$1/4$ cup white wine vinegar

12 ounces peeled shrimp (31 to 35 per pound)

$1/4$ cup extra virgin olive oil

1 shallot, thinly sliced

$1/4$ cup fresh lemon juice

1 tablespoon sugar

$1/4$ teaspoon sea salt

$1/4$ teaspoon freshly ground pepper

$1/4$ cup pine nuts, toasted

WHIPPED BACCALÀ WITH POLENTA CROSTINI

WHIPPED BACCALÀ WITH POLENTA CROSTINI This recipe is a fantastic way to introduce newcomers to delicious salt cod. Mellowed by onion, garlic, and olive oil, it is then whipped together with a little potato to make a creamy spread. Served on polenta crostini, this is a terrific starter with a glass of crisp white wine or chilled fino sherry.

Buy the salt cod in its dried state. Soak the cod in water in the refrigerator for 2 to 3 days, changing the water at least twice a day, to remove excess salt. Rinse the reconstituted fish and pat dry before cooking. • **MAKES 15 CROSTINI**

8 ounces salt cod, soaked (see above) and cut into 2-inch pieces

1 medium yellow potato, peeled and cut into 2-inch pieces

1 small onion, coarsely chopped

1 garlic clove, smashed and peeled

2 fresh rosemary sprigs

2 cups whole milk, or more to cover

Salt

3/4 cup yellow polenta

6 1/2 tablespoons extra virgin olive oil

Freshly ground white pepper

Combine the cod, potato, onion, garlic, and rosemary in a medium saucepan over low heat. Add enough milk to cover. Simmer, covered, until the potato is tender, about 30 minutes. Let cool.

Meanwhile, make the polenta crostini. Bring 1 quart water to a boil in a medium saucepan over medium-high heat. Add a pinch of salt and pour in the polenta, stirring constantly with a wooden spoon to prevent lumps from forming. Cook the polenta over low heat, stirring regularly, until smooth and creamy, 30 to 40 minutes.

Pour the polenta onto a lightly oiled sheet pan. With a spatula, shape into a 10 x 6-inch rectangle, approximately 1/2 inch thick. (The polenta molds easily as it cools.) When cooled completely, cut the polenta into 2-inch squares. The polenta can be covered and refrigerated for up to 2 days at this point. Before serving, warm the polenta crostini under the broiler on an oiled cookie sheet until browned. Set aside until ready to use.

To finish the baccalà, remove and discard the rosemary sprigs. Using a slotted spoon, transfer the cod, potatoes, onion, and garlic to a blender or food processor. Process until smooth, adding the olive oil and enough poaching liquid to make the cod creamy and smooth, the consistency of mashed potatoes. Taste and season with salt and pepper as needed. The cod can be refrigerated for up to 2 days. Warm in a saucepan over low heat before serving.

To serve, spread the warm whipped cod mixture on the polenta crostini.

GRILLED CHICKEN AND ROASTED TOMATO ON SEMOLINA BREAD

These hearty sandwiches are a delicious alternative to chicken salad or other chicken sandwiches. The time it takes to oven-roast the tomatoes is well worth it for the rich taste and texture they add. • **MAKES 16 PIECES**

6 plum tomatoes, cut in half lengthwise

Sea salt and freshly ground pepper

Four 5-ounce skinless, boneless chicken breast halves

5 tablespoons extra virgin olive oil

1 tablespoon balsamic vinegar

Small handful of baby spinach

Eight $1/2$-inch-thick slices semolina bread

Preheat the oven to 250°F.

Arrange the tomatoes cut side up on a cookie sheet and season with salt and pepper. Bake for about 6 hours, or until semisoft and dried. Let cool. Store in an airtight container in the refrigerator for up to a week.

Prepare a fire in a charcoal grill or preheat a gas grill to medium-high. Alternatively, preheat a grill pan over medium-high heat. Pound the chicken breasts between 2 sheets of plastic wrap until they are each $1/4$ inch thick. Brush with 2 tablespoons of the olive oil and season with salt and pepper. Grill until well marked and cooked through, about 2 minutes per side.

In a small mixing bowl, whisk together the balsamic vinegar and remaining 3 tablespoons olive oil with a pinch of salt and pepper to make a vinaigrette. Put the spinach in a medium bowl and toss with the vinaigrette until well coated.

Assemble the sandwiches by placing the chicken breasts on 4 of the bread slices. Top with the tomatoes and drizzle each tomato with a little vinaigrette. Top with the spinach and the remaining 4 bread slices. Cut into quarters and serve.

SHRIMP, ARUGULA, AND CAPER MAYONNAISE ON
BRIOCHE The traditional tea sandwiches of Venice are called *tramezzini* and are perfect for lunch, cocktail hour, or dinner. • **MAKES 16 PIECES**

Combine the egg yolk and capers in a medium mixing bowl. Mash with a fork to break up the capers slightly. Whisk in the lemon juice. Slowly whisk in the olive oil, drop by drop, increasing the flow to a slow, steady stream as the mixture starts to come together. Refrigerate for up to 1 day.

To serve, mix the shrimp and caper mayonnaise together and arrange on 4 of the brioche slices. Top with arugula and then the remaining 4 slices of brioche. Cut into quarters.

1 large egg yolk

1 tablespoon capers, preferably salted, rinsed

1 tablespoon fresh lemon juice

$1/2$ cup extra virgin olive oil

12 ounces cooked, peeled shrimp (31 to 35 per pound)

Eight $3/4$-inch-thick slices brioche bread, toasted

Small handful of arugula

SAUTÉED MUSHROOMS AND SWEET GARLIC WITH WHITE POLENTA

Polenta may have a longer history in Italy than either pasta or pizza. The first polenta was made with buckwheat that was brought to the area by the Saracens; today buckwheat polenta is still referred to as polenta Grano Saraceno. Then with the discovery of the New World, cornmeal replaced buckwheat flour.

In Venice you will find more dishes with white polenta than yellow, though either can be used here. This warm, comforting dish makes a lovely appetizer but can also be served as a side dish with a meat main course. • **SERVES 4 AS AN APPETIZER OR SIDE DISH**

4 garlic cloves, peeled

Sea salt and freshly ground black pepper

$1/2$ cup white polenta

1 tablespoon unsalted butter

$1/3$ cup grated montasio or fontina cheese

2 tablespoons extra virgin olive oil, plus more for drizzling

12 ounces mushrooms, preferably wild, such as chanterelles, morels, oyster, or shiitake, brushed clean and halved or quartered if large

$1/2$ cup low-sodium chicken broth

$1^{1}/2$ teaspoons chopped fresh rosemary leaves

Put the garlic cloves in a small saucepan and add enough water to cover. Bring to a boil over high heat and cook for 30 seconds. Drain and repeat. Drain the cloves once more and set aside.

Bring $2^{1}/3$ cups water to a boil in a large saucepan over medium heat. Add a pinch of salt and slowly pour in the polenta, stirring constantly with a wooden spoon to prevent lumps from forming. Reduce the heat to low and cook the polenta, stirring occasionally, until it loses its grainy texture and becomes smooth, about 40 minutes. Stir in the butter and cheese and season to taste with additional salt if necessary. Cover and keep warm.

Heat the olive oil in a large sauté pan over medium-high heat. Add the mushrooms and the blanched garlic cloves, cover, and cook for 1 minute. Turn the mushrooms over, replace the cover, and cook until the mushrooms are browned evenly, 2 to 3 minutes more. Add the broth and rosemary, season with salt and pepper, and cook, uncovered, until slightly reduced, about 30 seconds.

To serve, divide the polenta among 4 warmed shallow bowls. Spoon the mushrooms, garlic, and some of the pan juices over the polenta. Drizzle each serving with olive oil.

BLACK PASTA WITH SCUNGILLI AND TOMATO

BLACK PASTA WITH SCUNGILLI AND TOMATO Most of us think of conch as a Caribbean ingredient used in chowders and fritters, but scungilli, a cousin of the knobbed whelk, also resides in the southern Mediterranean. Often found in a marinated Sicilian salad, scungilli reaches new heights in this pasta dish.

The scungilli can be prepared ahead and refrigerated for up to 3 days or frozen for a month. Scungilli can be purchased fresh, already cooked and frozen, or canned; see the Resource Guide (page 194). For an equally delicious preparation, substitute squid for the scungilli. And while we like fresh pasta for this recipe, dried pasta works just as well.

● **SERVES 6 AS AN APPETIZER OR 4 AS A MAIN COURSE**

3 tablespoons extra virgin olive oil

3 garlic cloves, sliced

12 ounces frozen scungilli (conch), thawed, rinsed, and coarsely chopped, or 12 ounces cleaned squid, bodies cut into ¼-inch rings and tentacles left whole

½ cup dry white wine

One 24-ounce can tomato puree, preferably San Marzano

3 fresh thyme sprigs

Sea salt and freshly cracked black pepper

1 pound black (squid ink) linguine or fettuccine

Heat the olive oil in a medium sauté pan over medium heat. Add the garlic and cook until softened, 2 to 3 minutes. If using scungilli, add it to the pan and cook until the garlic is lightly browned, about 3 minutes. (The scungilli will not change color.) Add the wine and stir to scrape up any bits from the bottom of the pan. Add the tomato puree and thyme and season with salt and pepper. Cover and simmer until tender, 15 to 20 minutes.

If using squid, add it to the garlic in the pan, and cook until the squid becomes opaque, about 1 minute. Add the wine and stir to scrape up any bits from the bottom of the pan. Add the tomato puree and thyme and season with salt and pepper. Bring to a simmer and then turn off the heat.

Meanwhile, bring a large pot of lightly salted water to a boil. Add the pasta and cook until al dente, about 2 minutes less than what the directions advise. Drain the pasta and return to the pot. Ladle the sauce into the pot and toss the pasta over low heat for 2 minutes to marry it with the sauce. The pasta should still be slightly firm to the bite.

Divide among 6 warmed shallow bowls or plates and serve immediately.

AMARETTO POLENTA POUND CAKE

Classic American pound cake gets an Italian makeover when made with polenta and served with a drizzle of amaretto and a dollop of whipped cream. To bring this back into the American realm, as a variation, garnish with sliced bananas and caramel sauce. • **SERVES 8**

13 tablespoons unsalted butter, softened

1/2 cup plus 3 tablespoons yellow polenta

1 cup sugar

3 large eggs

4 large egg yolks

1/2 teaspoon almond extract

3/4 cup all-purpose flour

2 1/2 teaspoons baking powder

1/2 teaspoon salt

1/2 cup amaretto liqueur

Whipped cream, for garnish

Preheat the oven to 350°F. Grease a 9-inch loaf pan with 1 tablespoon of the butter and then dust the inside with the 3 tablespoons of polenta, tapping out the excess.

Put the sugar and remaining 12 tablespoons (1 1/2 sticks) butter in the bowl of an electric mixer fitted with the paddle attachment and beat on medium speed, scraping down the sides of the bowl as needed, until creamy and well blended, about 4 minutes. Add the eggs and egg yolks one at a time, beating well after each addition. Add the almond extract, beat for 30 seconds, and remove the bowl from the stand.

In a medium bowl, whisk together the flour, baking powder, remaining 1/2 cup polenta, and salt and fold into the egg mixture with a rubber spatula until combined.

Pour the batter into the prepared pan and bake for 40 minutes without opening the oven door. To test for doneness, insert a toothpick into the center of the cake: it should come out dry. Let the cake cool on a rack for 10 minutes before unmolding. Let cool to room temperature. The cake can be kept, well wrapped, for up to 2 days.

To serve, cut 8 slices of cake and lay each flat on a plate. Sprinkle each serving with a tablespoon of amaretto and top with a dollop of whipped cream.

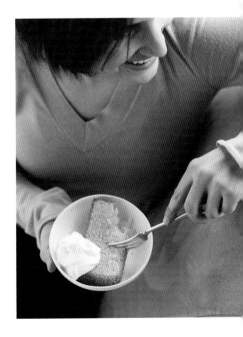

THE WINES OF THE VENETO, FRIULI–VENEZIA GIULIA, AND TRENTINO–ALTO ADIGE

THESE THREE NORTHEASTERNMOST REGIONS OF ITALY are often referred to as the Tre Venzie, or the Three Venices. This area produces high-quality white and red wines of style and substance.

Many wines are named after the grape type. Pinot Grigio, Pinot Bianco, Sauvignon Blanc, Chardonnay, Cabernet Franc, and Merlot have been growing there for centuries. Other native white wine grapes that we are now seeing more of in wines available in this country are the charismatic Tocai, the citrusy Ribolla Gialla, the floral Müller-Thurgau, and the concentrated Traminer, relative of Gewürztraminer. The cultural and language influences of Austria and Slovenia on one border and the Alps on the other have given this region of Italy some very Germanic-sounding wines.

Now that you know the names, let us tell you about some of our favorites.

Not as bracing as Pinot Grigio, Pinot Bianco has elegant peach and apple fruit flavors, light to medium body, with a clean, fresh finish, making it the perfect wine with fish. The best come from Friuli. Pinot Bianco is a delicious white cocktail wine that can stand up to a variety of flavors, from tart lemon to peppery arugula. Your "Chardonnay only" drinkers will love it.

An ideal white wine that is easy to drink though challenging to pronounce is Müller-Thurgau. It is a hybrid of Riesling and Sylvaner grapes, and its subtle tropical fruit flavors and fragrant aromas give this wine a sweet personality. Having a dry finish, Müller-Thurgau is a terrific wine for crudo and citrus flavors.

Not related to the Tokay from Alsace or Hungary, Tocai Friulano is a zesty and exotic white with excellent mineral undertones that make it pair nicely with oysters and other shellfish.

For red wines we recommend Lagrein, Teroldego, Valpolicella, and Amarone. Lagrein is a native grape that makes inky-colored robust wines and complements roasted meats and creamy cheeses. Teroldego is somewhat tannic, with hints of bitter chocolate and dried cherry, but is remarkable when enjoyed with slightly salty food like cured meats and baccalà.

The red wine star of the area is Amarone. Made from a blend of grapes left on the vine to ripen longer, then allowed to dry and concentrate for a few months before being pressed into wine, Amarone is powerful and earthy with flavors of violets, dark cherries, and licorice. Drunk with roasted meats and hearty cheeses, it also makes for a fine risotto. Amarone wines can be pricey, but younger grapes that don't make it to Amarone status go into making Valpolicella, which is an excellent value when made by Amarone producers.

All of the varietals from this area are worth seeking out. Some are easier to remember and pronounce than others, but you'll be rewarded for your efforts. They are satisfying, food-friendly wines that go well with a wide variety of foods. Look for producers Abbazia di Rosazzo, Allegrini, Alois Lageder, Boscaini, EnoFriulia, Foradori, Jermann, J. Hofstatter, Masi, Pieropan, Pojer e Sandri, Tiefenbrunner, and Zeni.

MILAN

WINE BAR ALLA MODA

THIS CHAPTER reflects the style of Europe's fashion capital, where haute couture is on display in the many stylish bars and restaurants in this economic hub of northern Italy.

Featuring recipes that are elegant yet easy, Milan inspires stylish sipping and modern munching. Milanese bars are also known for their elaborate cocktails and world-class champagne-method sparklers from the Franciacorta, a wine region just an hour away.

Negroni Sbagliato

Faux Gras (Vegetarian "Foie Gras")

Crispy Parmigiano Flatbread

Olive Oil Potato Chips with Sea Salt and Rosemary

Bresaola of Salmon with Lemon and Greens

Prosciutto with Grana, Shaved Artichokes, and Hearts of Palm

1662 Poached Capon Salad

Grilled Chicken Salad with Pesto, Raisins, Sun-Dried Tomatoes, and Pine Nuts

Ziti with Braised Veal

Barolo Risotto

Italian Almond Cake

The Wines of Lombardy and Piedmont

NEGRONI SBAGLIATO *Sbagliato* means "mistake" in Italian. The mistake in this drink is that the bartender at Bar Basso in Milan grabbed a bottle of sparkling wine instead of a bottle of gin to make a Negroni. The customer loved it. The rest is, of course, history.

Bar Basso is now known worldwide as the birthplace of this celebrated drink, but there's no need to wait for your next trip to Milan to taste it. • **MAKES 1 COCKTAIL**

Pour the Campari and vermouth into a cocktail shaker filled with ice, shake, and strain into a martini glass. Top off with the Prosecco.

1 ounce Campari

$1/2$ ounce sweet vermouth

$1^1/2$ ounces chilled Prosecco or other dry sparkling wine

FAUX GRAS (VEGETARIAN "FOIE GRAS") In Milan, we tasted a very convincing faux "foie gras" dish prepared at the creative vegetarian restaurant Joia. After we explained the dish to Effy Medrano, a great cook whom we have worked with for many years, he came up with this recipe in response to "The Great Chicago City Council Ban on Foie Gras of 2006." Serve this smooth spread on brioche toast.

Vin santo is a dessert wine from Tuscany that gives this dish just the right amount of sweetness. • **SERVES 6 AS AN APPETIZER**

Melt half of the butter in a medium sauté pan over medium-low heat. Add the onion and cook, stirring occasionally, until well caramelized, about 45 minutes. Add the capers and vin santo and stir to loosen the browned bits on the bottom of the pan. Continue to cook until the liquid has reduced by half, 2 to 3 minutes. Remove from the heat and allow the mixture to cool completely.

Transfer to a food processor and add the chickpeas and truffle oil. Puree into a paste. Add the remaining butter and puree until smooth. Season with salt and pepper.

Mound the puree in a serving bowl and chill for at least 2 hours and up to 24 hours before serving.

8 tablespoons (1 stick) unsalted butter

1 onion, thinly sliced

$3^1/2$ tablespoons capers, preferably salted, rinsed

$1/2$ cup vin santo or tawny port

Two 15-ounce cans chickpeas, drained

1 teaspoon white truffle oil

Sea salt and freshly ground black pepper

CRISPY PARMIGIANO FLATBREAD

CRISPY PARMIGIANO FLATBREAD This cheesy flatbread is so satisfyingly crunchy and easy to make that you will want to bake it regularly. We recommend using a manual or electric pasta machine to roll out the dough for these crispy, paper-thin treats. Using a rolling pin will yield slightly thicker results. After just one bite you will understand why this is one of the most sought-after recipes in our restaurants. • **MAKES 16 LARGE PIECES**

2 envelopes active dry yeast

1½ cups warm water

2 tablespoons extra virgin olive oil, plus more for brushing

4 cups all-purpose flour, plus more for dusting

1 teaspoon sea salt

2 cups freshly grated Parmigiano-Reggiano cheese

Combine the yeast and warm water in a small bowl and let sit until bubbly, about 5 minutes. Stir in the olive oil.

Put the flour and salt in the bowl of an electric mixer fitted with the dough hook or in a large bowl. Pour in the yeast mixture and mix on low speed or with your hands until the water is absorbed and a shaggy dough is formed. Knead the dough on a lightly floured board until the dough is uniform and smooth, 2 to 3 minutes. It will be slightly sticky.

Divide the dough into 4 equal pieces and shape into balls. Dust with flour and place on a floured cookie sheet. Cover with plastic wrap and let the dough rise in a warm place until doubled in size, 1 to 2 hours.

Preheat the oven to 425°F.

Have ready 2 nonstick cookie sheets or grease regular cookie sheets with olive oil.

Working with one dough ball at a time (cover the remaining dough with a moist kitchen towel until ready to use), dust the ball with flour and flatten with your hand. Cut the dough in half and roll half the dough through a pasta machine with the rollers set midway apart. Dust the dough with flour if it becomes sticky. Reduce the space between the rollers one setting at a time until you have reached the last setting and the dough is a smooth, thin sheet. Transfer to a cutting board and cut in half on an angle into large pieces so that 2 will fit on a cookie sheet. The pieces should each be approximately 4 inches wide and 12 inches long. Roll and cut the remaining half in the same manner as the first.

Place the rolled dough on the cookie sheets. Brush lightly with olive oil, sprinkle with about a quarter of the cheese, and bake until golden brown, 12 to 14 minutes. Let cool on a rack before serving. Repeat this process with the rest of the dough balls, rolling and baking until all the dough is used. Stored in an airtight container, the flatbread will keep for up to 2 days.

OLIVE OIL POTATO CHIPS WITH SEA SALT AND ROSEMARY

When we started traveling in Europe, we made Milan our home base. There we spent much of our time in wine bars, planning the day's activities and subsequent trips. After a while we became regulars at a small wine bar near our hotel. The staff got to know us and took great care of us whenever we stopped in. They also served the best homemade potato chips as a bar snack. Light and crispy, those chips were unlike any we'd ever had. Enjoying them with a glass of Franciacorta sparkling wine, grown and produced just outside Milan, became one of our fondest wine and food memories. See photograph on page 16. • **SERVES 4 TO 6**

2 large Idaho baking potatoes, unpeeled

2 quarts extra virgin olive oil

Sea salt

2 tablespoons finely chopped fresh rosemary leaves

Have ready a large bowl of cold water.

Using a mandoline, food processor, or sharp knife, carefully cut the potatoes into thin slices. Submerge them in the cold water and let sit for 1 hour.

Drain the potato slices well and pat dry with paper towels. Divide into 4 batches.

Heat the olive oil in a deep-fryer or heavy-bottomed pot until it reaches 335°F.

Add one batch of potato slices to the oil and cook, stirring from time to time, until the chips are browned evenly, 10 to 12 minutes. Carefully remove the chips from the oil using a slotted spoon and drain them on paper towels. While still hot, sprinkle with salt and 1½ teaspoons of the rosemary.

Repeat with the remaining potato slices, making sure to return the oil to 335°F between batches.

Serve warm or at room temperature.

BRESAOLA OF SALMON WITH LEMON AND GREENS

Using the traditional spice blend for bresaola, the famous Italian cured beef that comes from the Valtellina, north of Milan, you can make an Italian-inspired salmon gravlax. Choose the thickest fillet you can find for this easy to make and serve recipe. • **SERVES 6 AS AN APPETIZER**

In a shallow plastic or glass container just large enough for the salmon to fit snugly, combine the salt, sugars, cloves, cinnamon, pepper, and garlic. Nestle the salmon on top, pushing it down into the curing mixture. Pat the mixture around the sides of the fish, sprinkling a little from the sides onto the top. Cover and put in the refrigerator to cure for 24 hours. Flip the salmon over and return it to the refrigerator for another 24 hours.

To serve, remove the salmon from the container and scrape off any of the dry ingredients. Thinly slice the salmon into at least 12 equal pieces. Divide among 6 plates and top with the greens. Drizzle the olive oil and squeeze lemon juice over each serving.

$^3/_4$ cup kosher salt

$^1/_2$ cup (packed) light brown sugar

$^1/_4$ cup granulated sugar

$^1/_8$ teaspoon ground cloves

$^1/_2$ teaspoon ground cinnamon

1 tablespoon coarsely cracked black peppercorns

1 garlic clove, finely chopped

1 pound skinned salmon fillet

Handful of baby greens (optional)

2 tablespoons extra virgin olive oil

1 lemon

PROSCIUTTO WITH GRANA, SHAVED ARTICHOKES, AND HEARTS OF PALM

When Neil Empson, the renowned Italian wine importer, took us to his favorite restaurant in Milan, named after a famous racehorse, we were very curious. The *prosciutto lavorato,* a delicious salad of artichokes, hearts of palm, and shaved cheese with a lemon vinaigrette served over paper-thin slices of prosciutto, won us over and has become a favorite at our house ever since. ● **SERVES 4 AS AN APPETIZER**

To make the vinaigrette, squeeze 3 tablespoons lemon juice from the lemon, reserving the lemon, and put the juice in a medium bowl. Add the salt and pepper. In a slow stream, drizzle in the olive oil, whisking constantly until the vinaigrette is well blended. Set aside.

Fill a medium bowl with cold water. Squeeze any remaining juice from the lemon halves into the water and add the lemon halves too. Cut off all but 1 inch of the stem from each artichoke and then cut off the top fourth of each artichoke. Bend back and snap off the dark green outer leaves at the base until only the pale green and yellow leaves remain. Peel the stems with a vegetable peeler or paring knife to remove the tough outer layer. Cut each artichoke in half lengthwise. Using the point of a knife, remove any purple-tipped leaves or fuzzy choke from the center.

Using a mandoline, a ceramic handheld slicer, or a very sharp knife, carefully shave the artichokes into thin slices, starting with the flat side of the artichoke. Place the artichoke slices in the lemon water.

Shave or thinly slice the heart of palm and then the cheese.

Drain the artichokes and place on paper towels to dry.

To serve, place 2 slices of prosciutto on each of 4 plates. Add the artichokes, heart of palm, cheese, and arugula to the bowl with the vinaigrette and toss to coat. Divide the mixture among the plates, placing a portion on top of the prosciutto. Offer freshly ground pepper at the table.

1 small lemon, cut in half

Pinch of sea salt

Pinch of freshly ground white pepper, plus more for serving

½ cup plus 1 tablespoon extra virgin olive oil

2 baby artichokes

1 fresh heart of palm

4 ounces Grana Padano cheese

Handful of arugula

8 thin slices prosciutto

1662 POACHED CAPON SALAD

When we lived in Italy, we worked at Albergo del Sole, a restaurant just outside Milan. The owner, Franco Colombani, was an avid collector of old cookbooks. He became famous for reintroducing this recipe, which had originally been printed in 1662. Here is our interpretation.

If you can't find capon, substitute 1½ pounds chicken or turkey breast, keeping in mind that, depending on the size, the chicken will take less time to cook and the turkey will take about the same time as the capon. • **SERVES 4**

FOR THE CAPON

3 cups low-sodium chicken broth

½ cup extra virgin olive oil

2 garlic cloves, smashed

Two 12-ounce skinless, boneless capon breast halves

FOR THE SALAD

3 tablespoons extra virgin olive oil

1 tablespoon balsamic vinegar

Sea salt and freshly ground white pepper

½ head of frisée, heart leaves only

Handful of baby greens

3 tablespoons golden raisins, plumped in warm water and drained

3 tablespoons coarsely chopped almonds, preferably Marcona

½ medium carrot, cut into matchsticks

2 tablespoons thinly sliced citron (optional)

To poach the capon, bring the chicken broth, olive oil, and garlic to a simmer in a medium saucepan over medium heat. Place the capon in the stock. Simmer for 3 minutes. Do not boil. Flip the breasts over, cover, and turn off the heat. Let the capon sit in the warm stock for 15 minutes, or until an instant-read thermometer registers 150°F when inserted into the thickest part. Transfer to a plate and let rest for 5 minutes or refrigerate in the poaching liquid for up to 3 days. The capon can be served warm or chilled.

To make the vinaigrette for the salad, whisk together the olive oil, vinegar, and salt and pepper to taste in a small bowl.

To serve, slice each capon breast crosswise on a diagonal into ¼-inch slices. Transfer to a large bowl and combine with the frisée, baby greens, raisins, almonds, carrot, and citron if using it. Dress with half the vinaigrette, season with salt and pepper, and toss to coat. Divide the salad among 4 plates, topping each portion with capon slices. Drizzle each serving with the remaining vinaigrette.

GRILLED CHICKEN SALAD WITH PESTO, RAISINS, SUN-DRIED TOMATOES, AND PINE NUTS
This is a very satisfying chicken salad. The sweetness of the raisins and pine nuts, combined with the tartness of sun-dried tomatoes and the earthiness of pesto and grilled chicken, tastes great in the summer with a glass of crisp white wine. • **SERVES 6 AS AN APPETIZER OR 4 AS A MAIN COURSE**

Four 6-ounce skinless, boneless chicken breast halves

1 tablespoon extra virgin olive oil

Sea salt and freshly ground black pepper

Pesto (recipe follows)

1/3 cup raisins, plumped in warm water and drained

1/2 cup diced sun-dried tomatoes

1/4 cup pine nuts, toasted

Prepare a fire in a charcoal grill or preheat a gas grill to medium-high.

Coat the chicken breasts with the olive oil and season with salt and pepper. Arrange on the grill and cook until an instant-read thermometer registers 165°F when inserted into the thickest part, 3 to 4 minutes on each side.

Remove from the grill and set aside to cool. When cool enough to handle, thinly slice the breasts. Transfer to a large mixing bowl and add the pesto, raisins, sun-dried tomatoes, and pine nuts. Mix well to combine. Season to taste with salt and pepper. Serve or store covered in the refrigerator for up to a day. Remove from the refrigerator and let sit at room temperature for 30 minutes before serving.

PESTO
MAKES 1 CUP

2 cups loosely packed fresh basil leaves

1 garlic clove, peeled

3 tablespoons pine nuts

1/2 teaspoon sea salt

2/3 cup freshly grated Parmigiano-Reggiano cheese

1/4 cup extra virgin olive oil

Combine the basil, garlic, pine nuts, and salt in a blender or food processor. Process until pureed. Pour into a large mixing bowl and add the cheese and olive oil, stirring until the pesto is smooth and creamy. The pesto can be kept in the refrigerator for up to 2 days. Bring to room temperature before serving.

ZITI WITH BRAISED VEAL

ZITI WITH BRAISED VEAL Milan is known for its braised veal dish *osso buco*. Instead of using veal shank, we have substituted meatier cuts. Whichever cut you use, braising makes the meat incredibly tender while creating a rich, meaty-flavored sauce that's perfect for pasta. • **SERVES 6 AS AN APPETIZER OR 4 AS A MAIN COURSE**

2 pounds veal cheeks, trimmed, or boneless veal shoulder, cut into 2-inch pieces

Sea salt and freshly ground black pepper

3 tablespoons extra virgin olive oil

1 yellow onion, chopped

2 garlic cloves, smashed and peeled

2 carrots, chopped

2 celery stalks, chopped

1 1/2 cups dry red wine

1 cup canned crushed plum tomatoes with their juices, preferably imported San Marzano

2 cups low-sodium chicken broth

1 fresh rosemary sprig

1 pound ziti

1 cup freshly grated Parmigiano-Reggiano cheese, plus more for serving

Preheat the oven to 350°F.

Generously season the veal with salt and pepper. Heat the olive oil in a large ovenproof pot or Dutch oven over medium-high heat. Add the meat and brown on all sides, turning once, about 12 minutes total. Transfer the meat to a plate and set aside.

Add the onion, garlic, carrots, and celery to the pot. Cook, stirring frequently, scraping up the brown bits from the bottom, until the vegetables soften and begin to brown, 8 to 10 minutes. Add the wine, tomatoes and their juices, and chicken broth and scrape again to release any remaining browned bits off the bottom of the pan. Bring to a boil and then reduce the heat to low. Add the rosemary and veal. Cover the pot tightly with a lid or heavy-duty aluminum foil, transfer to the oven, and braise for 2 1/2 hours, or until fork-tender. The veal can be refrigerated in its cooking liquid for up to 3 days. Reheat before proceeding.

Reduce the oven temperature to 170°F.

Using a slotted spoon, transfer the veal to an ovenproof platter, cover with foil, and keep warm in the oven. Strain the sauce into a bowl through a fine-mesh strainer, discarding the solids, and return the sauce to the pot. Simmer over medium-high heat until reduced to about 1 cup. Taste and adjust the seasoning. Keep warm over low heat.

Meanwhile, bring a large pot of salted water to a boil. Add the ziti to the pot and cook, stirring frequently, until the pasta is al dente, about 2 minutes less than what is recommended on the box.

Drain the pasta. Add the pasta to the sauce and heat over medium heat. Cook for 1 to 2 minutes to allow the pasta to marry with the sauce and absorb some of it. Stir in the Parmigiano-Reggiano cheese and season with salt and pepper to taste.

Transfer the pasta to a platter. Top with the veal and additional Parmigiano-Reggiano cheese. Serve immediately.

BAROLO RISOTTO Using the king of Italian red wine in making risotto may seem extravagant and expensive, but the results are worth it. This creamy purple risotto will be like no other risotto you have ever tasted. Did we mention that it also pairs very nicely with a glass of the king? • **SERVES 6 AS AN APPETIZER**

3½ cups low-sodium chicken broth

9 tablespoons unsalted butter

½ small onion, finely chopped

2 cups Arborio, Carnaroli, or Vialone Nano rice

2 cups Barolo or other hearty red wine

1 cup freshly grated Parmigiano-Reggiano cheese, plus more for serving

Sea salt and freshly ground black pepper

Bring the chicken broth to a simmer in a medium saucepan. Meanwhile, melt 3 tablespoons of the butter in a heavy-bottomed skillet or a medium pot over medium heat. Add the onion and cook without browning until softened, 3 to 4 minutes. Add the rice and cook, stirring continuously, until it is coated with the butter and onion, 1 minute. Add the wine and simmer, still stirring, until almost completely absorbed, a minute or two. Add the hot broth to the rice a ladleful at a time and simmer, stirring continuously and waiting until the liquid is almost completely absorbed before adding more broth.

When all of the liquid has been added and the rice is al dente, after about 20 minutes, remove the pot from the heat and stir in the remaining 6 tablespoons butter and the Parmigiano-Reggiano. Season with salt to taste.

Divide the risotto among 6 warmed shallow bowls. Sprinkle with additional Parmigiano and some pepper and serve immediately.

ITALIAN ALMOND CAKE

An old regional recipe from Lombardy, where it is known as *torta sbriciolona,* this cake or giant cookie sort of falls between the two. Its Italian name comes from the word *scriciolare,* which means "to crumble." We first enjoyed sbriciolona twenty years ago while living and working near Mantova at the restaurant Al Bersagliere, where the chef, Massimo Ferrari, taught us how to make it. Some years later, while visiting us in Chicago, Massimo shared his recipe with us. This cake keeps for several days. • **MAKES 8 TO 12 INDIVIDUAL CAKES**

Preheat the oven to 275°F.

Have ready eight 3-inch nonstick tartlet pans or grease 12 cups of a standard muffin tin.

Mix the flour, cornmeal, and baking powder together in a small bowl.

In a stand mixer fitted with the paddle attachment, beat the butter and sugar on high speed until pale, about 3 minutes. Add the egg yolks, vanilla, and lemon zest and continue to beat until thick, 2 to 3 minutes. Turn the mixer to low and add the almonds, followed by the dry ingredients. Mix slowly until just combined, about 1 minute. The dough will be crumbly and in pieces.

Mound the dough, pressing down a little, into the tartlet pans. The cakes should resemble little mountains. Bake until golden brown, about 45 minutes.

Remove from the tart pans and let cool on a wire rack. Before serving, dust the cakes with confectioners' sugar.

1 cup all-purpose flour

1/2 cup cornmeal

1 1/2 teaspoons baking powder

8 tablespoons (1 stick) unsalted butter, softened

3/4 cup granulated sugar

2 large egg yolks

1/4 teaspoon vanilla extract

1/4 teaspoon grated lemon zest

3/4 cup sliced almonds

Confectioners' sugar, for serving

THE WINES OF LOMBARDY
AND PIEDMONT

WHILE ALL OVER ITALY most wines are produced for everyday drinking, and that holds true for northern Italy as well, the wines of Lombardy and Piedmont are the ones perhaps with the most pedigree. Italians are proud of the world-class offerings from these two famous regions and, thank goodness, export them to shores as lucky as our own.

Franciacorta is a wine-growing area east of Milan that produces high-quality champagne-method sparkling wines of finesse and sophistication. These *spumante* are made predominantly with Chardonnay, Pinot Noir, Pinot Grigio, and Pinot Bianco grapes. The same terminology used to describe the level of sweetness in champagne is used for these wines—*nature, brut, extra dry*, and so on. Champagne-method sparklers from this region have been made only since the 1960s; these are delicious wines with excellent, creamy bubbles of personality and charm, ideal as cocktail wines but also satisfying with food. Serve a Franciacorta sparkler with chunks of Reggiano-Parmigiano cheese at your next dinner party and watch as your guests marvel at the pairing.

Look for wines from Bellavista, Ca'del Bosco, Cavalleri, and Contadi Castaldi.

Piemonte (Piedmont) is probably the best-known wine-producing region in Italy. It is most famous for its traditional red wines called Barolo and Barbaresco. Named after the villages where the Nebbiolo grapes are grown and made into these wines, these are powerful and distinctive age-worthy wines that mellow with time.

Wine and food are taken very seriously in this corner of the country. The villages of Barolo and Barbaresco surround the town of Alba, where one of nature's most prized gifts, white truffles, are harvested from late October through late December. They have an earthy aroma of ripe cheese and garlic. During truffle season, you can find truffles served in even the humblest of wine bars in the towns and villages near Alba, lovingly shaved over simple fried eggs or mashed potatoes. When you are ready to splurge, try fresh white truffles shaved over pasta or risotto with a glass of Barolo or Barbaresco wine and see for yourself just what all the reverential talk is about.

Barbera, Dolcetto, and other Nebbiolo-based wines grown in Alba and in the north of the region are the everyday drinking wines of Piemonte. Robust with dried-cherry fruit and spunky acidity, Barbera is a mouth-filling companion to food. Light in body with simply delicious grapy flavors, Dolcetto is unpretentious and easy to drink. Nebbiolos like Gattinara, Ghemme, and Spanna have dusty dryness and substantial tannins and are perfect with juicy roast meats or rustic, hearty pasta dishes. Nebbiolo from Alba falls between the robust and the refined. Good alternatives to the more expensive Barolo and Barbaresco, these are lighter and smoother wines than other inexpensive Nebbiolos. Great producers from these regions are Bologno, Ceretto, Conterno, Einaudi, Gaja, Giacosa, Marcarini, Mascarello, Pio Cesare, Prunotto, Ratti, Scavino, and Travaglini.

PROSCIUTTO
DI PARMA

PANCETTA

PROSCIUTTO
AMERICANO
(untrimmed)

CHORIZO

FUET

GALLEGO-
STYLE
CHORIZO

HANDCRAFTED ARTISANAL CURED MEATS

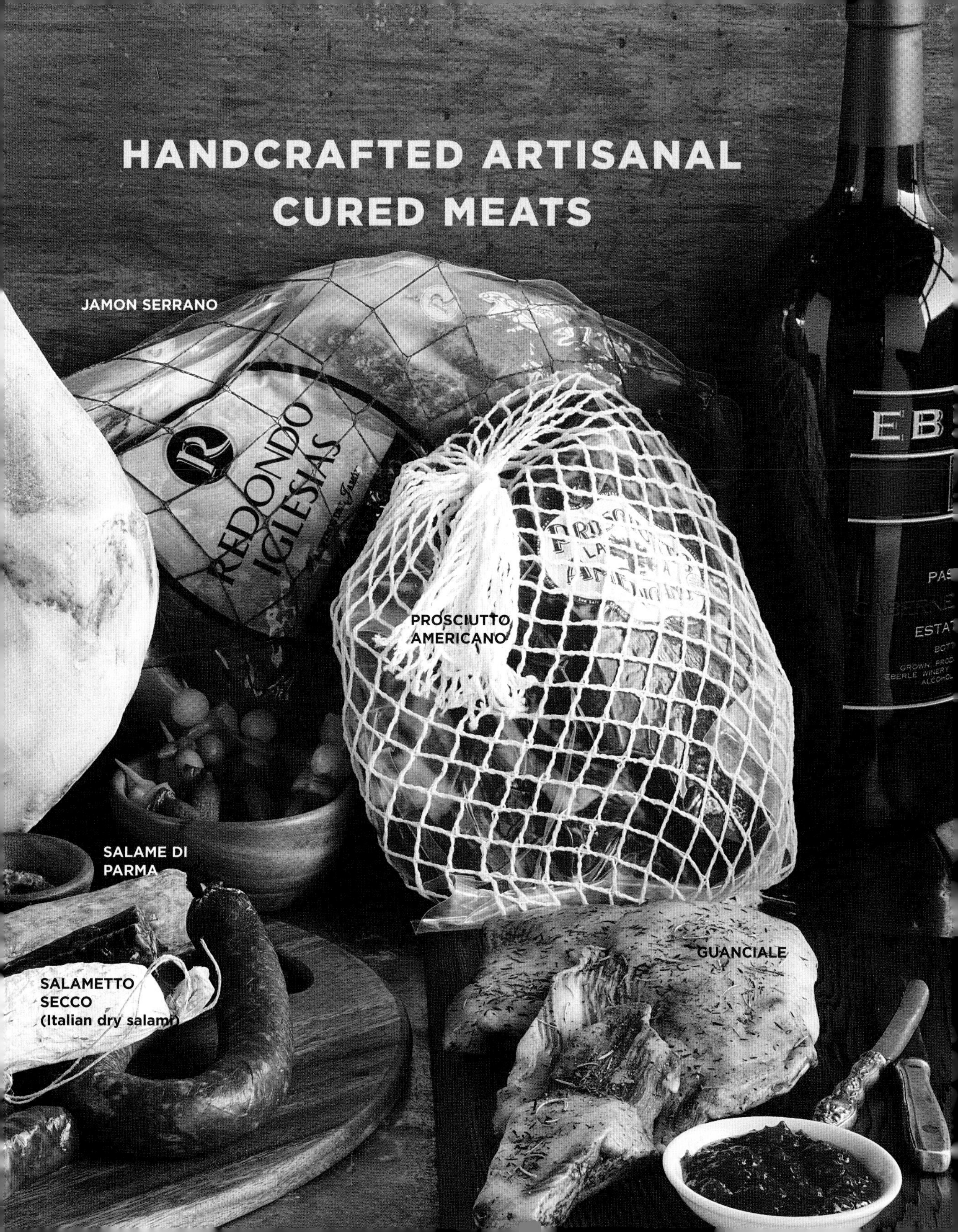

JAMON SERRANO

PROSCIUTTO
AMERICANO

SALAME DI
PARMA

SALAMETTO
SECCO
(Italian dry salami)

GUANCIALE

AN IMPORTANT PART OF ANY WINE BAR MENU is the selection of cured meats. Served individually or as part of an assortment, traditionally prepared meats offer a variety of textures and flavors. Great with many different wines, cured meats satisfy and are easy to serve.

Handcrafted meats created by artisans have become some of the most sought-after food products today. There is a real skill to this craft, and it begins with the highest-quality pork. Until recently the best products were imported and quite limited due to restrictions imposed by the U.S. government. Now restrictions have been eased and more products have become available to the American consumer.

Just as encouraging, American farmers are now raising more quality pork that is breed specific and is not as lean as commercially raised pork, which makes it perfect for European-style cured meat products. Consequently, American artisan salumi and prosciutto makers are producing salami, coppa, lardo, pancetta, and prosciutto from these tastier breeds.

Not that any of this is all that new; it's more of an example of a culture coming full circle. In the early twentieth century, Italian immigrants made their own cured meats based on traditional recipes and flavors of the regions they left behind. Years later, as these immigrants assimilated into everyday American life and melting-pot culture, these traditions were forgotten.

Now in markets across the country, you find not only Italian-inspired cured meats but also products from Spain, France, and Portugal, to name just a few.

When making your own cured meat platter at home, select the meats for variety. Offer a tasting of three to five different cuts, thinly sliced. We recommend a few slices of each per person. When serving salumi or chorizo in the traditional link shape, you may want to slice a few pieces and place the slices and the links on a cutting board with a knife to allow people to help themselves. This way the meat won't dry out. For accompaniments, all you really need are some crispy breadsticks or crusty bread and perhaps some marinated olives and vegetables. And don't forget the red wine!

PANCETTA is unsmoked pork belly bacon cured with black pepper and other spices. While not often eaten raw, it is cooked in many pasta dishes, the best known being spaghetti carbonara and amatriciana. It is also used in the recipe for Porchetta Panini (page 55).

SPECK (not pictured) is smoked prosciutto, cured with garlic, black pepper, and juniper berries. *Speck* is the German word for bacon, and the ham originates in the Sud Tirol, the very northern part of Italy. It is delicious with Alpine cheeses such as fontina.

PROSCIUTTO AMERICANO (untrimmed) is similar to Italian prosciutto in that it has a decent amount of fat. It is smaller than the other prosciutto Americano featured in this picture and the closest to Italian-made ham that we have found in the United States. It is made in Iowa by La Quercia. (See the Resource Guide, page 194.)

PROSCIUTTO DI PARMA, the glorious ham from Emilia-Romagna, is government sanctioned as a Denominazione di Origine Protetta product, which means it is an "agricultural and food product whose properties are essentially or exclusively derived from their geographical environment, inclusive of natural and human factors, and whose production, transformation and processing are effected in the place of origin." Look for the DOP marking with the distinctive crown logo.

Another famous Italian ham, PROSCIUTTO DI SAN DANIELE (not pictured) is a DOP product made in the same method as Parma ham, but it comes from Friuli in northeastern Italy. People debate which ham is better, but we like both. Prosciutto should be slightly salty and faintly sweet. The best way to decide is to taste for yourself. Ask for a taste of each at the market before you buy, or better yet, stage your own prosciutto- and wine-tasting party.

Prosciutto should have red to pink flesh with a very white fat border. The aroma should be sweet and fragrant. To serve, have it sliced as thinly as possible. It is traditionally paired with fresh figs or melon, but we think it is best on its own.

JAMON SERRANO literally means "ham from the mountains" in Spanish, and it is now available in the United States. Compared with Italian prosciutto, this ham will have a firmer, drier texture that results in a more intense flavor. Thinly sliced, it's always a favorite on our cured meat platter. Savor its many layers of flavor in Tomato Bread with Serrano Ham and Manchego Cheese (page 123).

PROSCIUTTO AMERICANO. This prosciutto (pictured) is also made in Iowa by our friends at La Quercia from pigs raised humanely and without antibiotics and hormones. Serve this ham as you would prosciutto on your next cured meat platter.

GUANCIALE is the cured pork jowl "bacon" that is often used for cooking. It is very similar to pancetta, and purists say it should be used instead of pancetta for many Italian dishes. Guanciale can be hard to find, but it is worth trying for its sweeter flavor.

SPANISH CHORIZO is distinctly flavored with smoked paprika and available in mild and hot varieties. Simply slice and serve.

SALAME DI PARMA, a fresh salami made in the hills around the city of Parma, is flavored with red wine and black peppercorns. Not aged as long as dried salami, it has a sweet taste and a rich, soft texture.

ITALIAN DRY SALAME is an aged hard salami. A mixture of pork and beef, and sometimes garlic, it is probably the most familiar salami of its type to American palates. It is delicious by itself or when served with olives and crusty bread.

GALLEGO-STYLE CHORIZO, seasoned with wine, smoked paprika, and sea salt, comes from Galicia in northwestern Spain. Traditionally cooked in stews and paella, this is what we use for the Portuguese soup Caldo Verde (page 169).

CHORIZO made in the States is ready to eat and also seasoned with smoked paprika.

FUET is made from pork and is an aged dry-style salami from Catalonia, Spain. Very mild in flavor, it can be grilled or cooked in soups.

FLORENCE

ENOTECA TOSCANA

THE RUSTIC SIMPLICITY of the food found in local wine bars in and around Florence is the perfect match for the great wines produced from the surrounding hills. Here we have chosen dishes to pair with the famous wines of Tuscany and Umbria. Also, discover in these pages how these wines are used in recipes for added depth and flavor.

Red Grape Focaccia

Baked Caciocavallo Cheese

Onion Bread Soup

Spinach Salad with Crispy Shallots

Crespelle with Ricotta and Tomato Sauce

Trout with Roasted Artichokes, Shallots, and Giant White Beans

Steak Tagliata with Arugula

Sangiovese-Marinated Italian Sausage with Peppers and Onions

Tuscan Braised Venison with Creamy Polenta

Porchetta Panini

Florentine-Style Tripe

The Wines of Umbria

RED GRAPE FOCACCIA This harvest focaccia is a perfect complement to any wine tasting or cheese plate. In Tuscany, this thicker grape-studded flatbread is called *schiacciata* and is made throughout the year, but it is most popular during the grape harvest in fall. See photograph on page 41. • **MAKES FORTY 2-INCH-SQUARE PIECES**

2 envelopes active dry yeast

Pinch of sugar

2 cups warm water

1/4 cup plus 2 tablespoons extra virgin olive oil, plus more for brushing

5 cups all-purpose flour

2 teaspoons sea salt, plus salt for sprinkling

12 ounces red seedless grapes

Combine the yeast, sugar, and water in a small bowl and let sit until bubbly, about 5 minutes. Stir in 2 tablespoons of the olive oil.

Put the flour and salt in the bowl of an electric mixer fitted with the dough hook. Pour in the yeast mixture and mix on low speed until the dough pulls away from the sides of the bowl, 3 to 5 minutes.

Transfer the sticky dough to a generously floured 6-inch-square section of a counter or board. Dust the dough liberally with flour, patting the dough to form a rectangle. Let the dough sit for 5 minutes.

Dust your hands with flour and stretch the dough in each direction to twice its size. Fold the dough over itself in three, letter style, and form a rectangle. Brush the dough with 1 tablespoon of olive oil, dust with flour, and loosely cover with plastic wrap. Let sit for 1 hour.

Meanwhile, line a standard 11 x 17-inch rimmed cookie sheet with parchment paper. Drizzle the remaining 3 tablespoons of olive oil over the parchment and spread it to cover.

Transfer the dough to the cookie sheet with a plastic scraper or spatula, trying to retain the rectangular shape as much as possible. Flip the dough over and use your fingertips to stretch the dough until it fits inside the pan. Distribute the grapes across the dough, pushing them in slightly. Put the dough in a warm place to rise for 1 hour. Alternatively, the dough can be covered loosely with plastic wrap and refrigerated for up to 3 days. Remove the pan from the refrigerator 3 hours before baking.

Preheat the oven to 500°F.

Lightly brush the dough with olive oil and sprinkle with salt. Place the pan in the oven, lower the temperature to 450°F, and bake for 10 minutes. Rotate the pan 180 degrees and continue baking the focaccia until it begins to turn a light golden brown, 10 to 15 minutes. Remove from the oven and transfer to a wire rack. Carefully peel off the parchment if necessary. Cool for at least 20 minutes before slicing and serving.

BAKED CACIOCAVALLO CHEESE On a recent trip to Italy, our friend Janice Goldsmith sampled this dish in restaurants all over Tuscany. She couldn't stop raving about how simple it was to make and how satisfying it was. We couldn't wait for our next trip to sample it, so we began experimenting at home instead. Here is the fruit of our delicious labor: a bubbly, melted, gooey extravaganza akin to an ultraeasy version of fondue. It is essential to serve this with plenty of crusty bread.

Rich and buttery textured, caciocavallo is a deliciously sharp and tangy cow's milk cheese. Readily available in Italian markets, caciocavallo is gourd shaped and tied with a rope that loops around the "neck." • **SERVES 6 TO 8 AS AN APPETIZER**

2 tablespoons extra virgin olive oil

1 pound caciocavallo or provolone cheese, wax removed, cut into 1/2-inch slices

Leaves of 8 fresh herb sprigs— 2 rosemary, 2 sage, 2 thyme, and 2 parsley—or 8 slices black truffle

Preheat the oven to 375°F.

Pour the olive oil into the bottom of an ovenproof 10-inch baking dish. Arrange the cheese in an even layer in the dish and scatter the herbs on top. Bake until the cheese is soft and gooey, about 25 minutes. Serve immediately from the oven.

ONION BREAD SOUP Tuscans have a magical way with day-old bread. In fact, there are several recipes that call for stale bread in this region. This nourishing soup happens to be our favorite, not just because it's so warming and satisfying but also because it's a good example of the Italian knack for creating something great with simple ingredients. • **SERVES 6 TO 8 AS AN APPETIZER**

3 tablespoons extra virgin olive oil, plus more for drizzling

5 large sweet onions, thinly sliced

Sea salt and freshly ground black pepper

½ cup dry red wine

2 quarts low-sodium beef broth

1 (4- to 5-inch) piece of Parmigiano-Reggiano cheese rind (optional)

One 1-pound loaf crusty country-style bread

Freshly grated Parmigiano-Reggiano cheese, for garnish and serving

Heat the oil in a large pot over low heat. Add the onions, season with salt and pepper, and stir well to coat. Cook slowly, stirring occasionally, until the onions are golden brown and translucent, about 2 hours.

Turn the heat up to medium-high and add the wine, stirring to release any browned bits from the bottom of the pot. Add the broth and the Parmigiano rind and bring to a boil. Reduce the heat and simmer for 30 minutes. Remove the rind from the soup. The soup can be made to this point and refrigerated for up to 2 days. Reheat before proceeding.

Meanwhile, preheat the oven to 200°F.

Remove the crust from the bread and discard. Cut the bread into 2-inch pieces (about 6 cups) and scatter in an even layer on a cookie sheet. Bake until lightly toasted, about 30 minutes. Remove from the oven and set aside.

Add the bread to the soup and stir well to combine. Bring to a boil and simmer for 15 minutes. Stir again, season with salt and pepper, and adjust the consistency with a little broth or water if the soup seems too thick.

To serve, ladle the soup into warm bowls. Drizzle with olive oil and garnish with Parmigiano-Reggiano. Serve immediately, passing more Parmigiano-Reggiano and pepper at the table.

SPINACH SALAD WITH CRISPY SHALLOTS

SPINACH SALAD WITH CRISPY SHALLOTS The shallots should be cooked long and slow and will add the right amount of sweetness and crunch to the salad. • **SERVES 4 AS AN APPETIZER OR A SIDE DISH**

Preheat the oven to 250°F.

Heat 2 tablespoons of the oil in a medium sauté pan over medium heat. Add the shallots and cook, stirring occasionally, until caramelized, 15 to 20 minutes. Drain the shallots on paper towels and then spread evenly on a cookie sheet. Bake until crispy, about 30 minutes. Set aside to cool.

Whisk the vinegar with a pinch of salt and a pinch of pepper in a large bowl. In a slow stream, drizzle in the remaining ½ cup oil, whisking constantly until the vinaigrette is well blended. Add the spinach to the bowl and toss to combine. Season with salt and pepper to taste.

Divide the spinach among 4 chilled plates, sprinkle the shallots on top, and serve immediately.

½ cup plus 2 tablespoons extra virgin olive oil

4 medium shallots, thinly sliced and separated into rings

3 tablespoons red wine vinegar

Sea salt and freshly ground black pepper

6 ounces fresh spinach, stems removed

CRESPELLE WITH RICOTTA AND TOMATO SAUCE *Crespelle*

means "crepes" in Italian, and these are often served as a savory rather than a sweet. When filled with ricotta and baked, they remind us of a pasta dish, only lighter. These cheese-filled pouches are just as flavorful at room temperature as they are hot out of the oven. • **SERVES 6 AS AN APPETIZER OR 3 TO 4 AS A MAIN COURSE**

Two 16-ounce containers (4 cups) ricotta cheese

2¼ cups freshly grated Parmigiano-Reggiano cheese

3 tablespoons chopped fresh parsley leaves

Sea salt and freshly ground black pepper

1½ cups all-purpose flour

3 large eggs

1½ cups milk

3 tablespoons unsalted butter, melted and cooled

Olive oil, for cooking the crespelle

Tomato Sauce (recipe follows) or one 24-ounce jar store-bought tomato sauce

Scoop the ricotta cheese into a strainer set over a large bowl and drain overnight in the refrigerator.

Combine the drained ricotta with 1¼ cups of the Parmigiano, the parsley, and salt and pepper to taste in a large mixing bowl. Mix well and refrigerate until ready to use or for up to 24 hours.

To make the crespella batter, sift the flour into a large mixing bowl. Add the eggs and ½ cup of the milk and mix well. Slowly whisk in the remaining 1 cup milk. The batter should be fairly runny.

Add the melted butter and a generous pinch of salt and whisk for 2 minutes. Set the batter aside to rest for at least 1 hour at room temperature or overnight in the refrigerator.

To cook the crespelle, brush the bottom of a nonstick 10-inch pan with oil and place on the stove over medium heat. Rewhisk the batter gently and then ladle in 2 table-spoons of the batter, tilting the pan so the batter covers the bottom to form a round, thin layer. Cook the crespella until the underside is set and golden, 2 to 3 minutes. (Run a spatula around the edge and slightly lift the spatula to see the underside of the crespella.) Flip over with a spatula and cook the second side of the crespella for 1 to 2 minutes. Slide the crespella out of the pan onto a plate and repeat the process until all the batter is used, stacking the crespelle on top of one another. Alternatively, stack the crespelle between sheets of parchment, cover with plastic wrap, and store in the refrigerator for up to 24 hours.

Preheat the oven to 375°F.

Ladle 1 cup tomato sauce into a 13 x 9-inch baking dish.

Place 2 heaping tablespoons of the ricotta filling in the middle of each crespella and fold the top of the crespella to the bottom, patting lightly, forming a half circle. Fold in half again to make a triangle. Place the filled crespella in the pan.

Repeat this process, laying the crespelle slightly overlapping one another, until the pan is filled. Pour the remaining 2 cups tomato sauce over and around the crespelle. Sprinkle the remaining 1 cup Parmigiano cheese over the top. Tightly covered with plastic, the crespelle can be refrigerated overnight and baked the next day.

Bake until browned and bubbling, 20 minutes. Serve warm or let cool to room temperature.

TOMATO SAUCE
MAKES ABOUT 3 CUPS

Heat the olive oil in a medium saucepan over medium-high heat. Add the garlic and brown on both sides, 2 to 3 minutes. To avoid splattering, reduce the heat to low and add the tomato puree and 1 cup water. Turn up the heat and bring to a simmer. Cook until slightly reduced, about 20 minutes. Remove from the heat and stir in the basil leaves. The sauce can be refrigerated for up to 3 days. Reheat before using.

3 tablespoons extra virgin olive oil

2 garlic cloves, peeled and smashed

One 24-ounce jar or can tomato puree, preferably San Marzano

Sea salt and freshly ground black pepper

4 fresh basil leaves

TROUT WITH ROASTED ARTICHOKES, SHALLOTS, AND GIANT WHITE BEANS

TROUT WITH ROASTED ARTICHOKES, SHALLOTS, AND GIANT WHITE BEANS The combination of crispy artichokes, caramelized shallots, and roasted beans tastes terrific with trout. If you prepare the beans and vegetables first, the dish finishes quickly and easily.

Fresh rainbow trout is readily available all over the States and is a widely overlooked yet reasonably priced fish with delicious sweet flesh. ● **SERVES 4 AS AN APPETIZER OR 2 AS A MAIN COURSE**

½ cup dried giant white beans

2 large artichokes

5 tablespoons extra virgin olive oil, plus more for drizzling

8 small shallots, peeled and halved

2 fresh rosemary sprigs

Sea salt and freshly ground black pepper

Four 4-ounce trout fillets

1 lemon, cut into wedges

Put the beans in a medium bowl, add water to cover by about 4 inches, and let soak for 6 hours or overnight.

Drain the beans and transfer to a small saucepan, add enough water to cover by 2 inches, and place over medium heat. Bring to a boil and cook until tender, 45 to 60 minutes. Drain and set aside to cool.

Preheat the oven to 450°F.

Meanwhile, trim the artichokes as described on page 25, cutting the halves into 4 wedges each. As the artichokes will be roasted and browned, there is no need to drop them into lemon water.

Drizzle 3 tablespoons of the olive oil over a rimmed cookie sheet. Put the oiled pan into the oven to heat for 5 minutes. Carefully add the shallots, artichokes, beans, and rosemary to the hot pan. Season with salt and pepper, toss together, and transfer the pan to the preheated oven. Roast, stirring once or twice, until everything is golden brown and the artichokes and shallots are cooked through, about 20 minutes. Remove from the oven and set aside while you cook the fish. Keep the oven on.

Heat the remaining 2 tablespoons olive oil in a large ovenproof sauté pan over high heat until near smoking. Season the trout fillets with salt and pepper and carefully add them to the pan, skin side up. Cook for 2 to 3 minutes, then flip the trout over and transfer it to the oven. Turn the oven off and roast for 1 minute. The fish should look opaque throughout when prodded with a fork.

To serve, place the fillets skin side down on each of 4 warmed plates. Divide the roasted vegetables equally on top of the fish, discarding the rosemary sprigs. Drizzle each serving with olive oil and a squeeze of lemon.

STEAK TAGLIATA WITH ARUGULA

Tagliata means "sliced" in Italian and denotes the most popular way of serving steak in Tuscany. Charred first, then sliced and put on a serving plate, the meat is drizzled with the finest olive oil, making a sauce with the warm meat juices.

Arugula's peppery, nutty flavor cuts through the meat's richness, and rosemary and lemon help round out the dish. Be sure not to squeeze the lemon directly onto the meat, or it will discolor. • **SERVES 4 AS AN APPETIZER OR 2 AS A MAIN COURSE**

Prepare a fire in a charcoal grill or preheat a gas grill to medium-high.

Generously season the beef with salt and pepper. Arrange on the grill and sear, turning once, until an instant-read thermometer inserted into the thickest part registers 120°F, or medium rare, 3 to 4 minutes on each side.

Remove from the grill. Transfer to a cutting board and let the meat rest for 5 minutes. Slice the steak against the grain on an angle into 10 to 12 pieces. Arrange the slices down the middle of a warm serving platter and place the arugula on each side. Sprinkle the meat with olive oil and rosemary. Squeeze the lemon over the arugula and drizzle with some olive oil. Serve hot.

One 12-ounce strip steak, trimmed of any fat or sinew

Sea salt and freshly cracked black pepper

Small handful of arugula

Extra virgin olive oil

1 teaspoon chopped fresh rosemary

¼ lemon

SANGIOVESE-MARINATED ITALIAN SAUSAGE WITH PEPPERS AND ONIONS

When made into wine, the Sangiovese grape goes by many names: Brunello, Morellino, Prugnolo, Vino Nobile, and sometimes even "the blood of Jupiter." Marinating sausages in the wine gives them a sophisticated flavor, while the sweetness of the peppers and onions brings out the fruitiness of the wine.

• **SERVES 6 AS A TASTING PORTION, 4 AS AN APPETIZER, OR 2 AS A MAIN COURSE**

1 pound sweet Italian sausage links (about 4)

1½ cups Sangiovese or other dry, fruity red wine

2 tablespoons extra virgin olive oil

1 red bell pepper, cut into chunks

1 green bell pepper, cut into chunks

2 small onions, peeled and cut into chunks

3 garlic cloves, smashed and peeled

Cut the sausage links into 12 equal pieces total. Place in a baking dish small enough to hold the pieces snugly, and pour in the wine, making sure it completely covers the sausages. Marinate in the refrigerator for at least 12 and up to 24 hours.

Preheat the oven to 400°F.

Remove the sausage pieces from the marinade and pat dry with paper towels. Discard the marinade.

Heat a 3-quart baking dish in the oven for 3 minutes. Add the olive oil, sausages, red and green bell peppers, onions, and garlic to the dish and roast, turning once, until the sausages are cooked through and lightly browned, 25 to 30 minutes.

Remove from the oven and arrange on a serving platter or plates. Serve immediately.

TUSCAN BRAISED VENISON WITH CREAMY POLENTA This

comforting winter recipe is inspired by the many hearty dishes we've enjoyed in restaurants from the wine-producing areas of Tuscany.

For a variation, substitute beef shoulder or chuck stew meat for the venison. For an even more authentic Tuscan experience, try substituting boar for the venison. • **SERVES 6 AS AN APPETIZER OR 4 AS A MAIN COURSE**

Combine the garlic, onion, bay leaves, and wine in a nonreactive shallow pan. Add the venison and turn to coat. Cover and refrigerate for 24 hours.

The next day, preheat the oven to 350°F.

Remove the meat from the marinade and pat dry with paper towels. Reserve the marinade and vegetables. Season the meat generously with salt and pepper.

Heat the olive oil in a Dutch oven or medium ovenproof pot over medium-high heat. Add the marinated garlic, then the venison, and sear well, browning the meat on all sides, 8 to 10 minutes. Add the tomatoes and juice and scrape the browned bits off the bottom of the pan. Add the rosemary and the reserved marinade and remaining vegetables. Bring to a simmer, cover, and place in the oven. Cook until fork-tender, about 2 hours. Taste and season with salt and pepper if needed. Discard the bay leaves and the rosemary sprig. The venison can be cooked to this point and refrigerated for up to 3 days or frozen for up to 1 month. Reheat before proceeding.

When the venison is nearly fork-tender, mix the polenta, cream, and ³/₄ cup water together in a medium saucepan. Bring to a simmer, stirring constantly with a wooden spoon. Continue to cook and stir the polenta until it loses its grainy texture and is smooth, about 20 minutes. Add the butter and Parmigiano cheese and stir until well incorporated. Season to taste with salt and pepper.

Serve immediately with the venison.

4 garlic cloves, smashed and peeled

1 small onion, coarsely chopped

2 bay leaves

2 cups dry red wine

2 pounds boneless venison leg or stew meat, cut into 1-inch pieces

Sea salt and freshly ground black pepper

3 tablespoons extra virgin olive oil

One 28-ounce can whole tomatoes with juice, preferably San Marzano

1 fresh rosemary sprig

FOR THE POLENTA

1 cup white polenta

³/₄ cup heavy cream

2 tablespoons unsalted butter

¹/₃ cup freshly grated Parmigiano-Reggiano cheese

Sea salt and freshly ground white pepper

PORCHETTA PANINI All throughout Tuscany and Umbria you'll find certain piazzas brimming with parked trucks and crowds of all kinds of people surrounding them. It could be a Sunday afternoon, it could be 2:00 A.M., or it could be after a soccer game. These trucks are equipped with special ovens that cook porchetta: whole roasted pig, Tuscan style. Everyone is there to eat porchetta sandwiches standing up, with the sweet juices running over the paper wrapper onto their fingers.

This is our adaptation, using pork butt instead of a whole pig. The results are just as succulent but easy to pull off at home. Serve these sandwiches with mild and hot giardinera, an oil-and-vinegar-pickled vegetable mix that includes green and red bell peppers, carrots, cauliflower, olives, and peperoncini, and can be found in the Italian or pickle section of grocery stores. • **MAKES 8 SANDWICHES**

Have the butcher butterfly the pork butt into a rectangular shape approximately ³/₄ inch thick.

Mix the fennel seeds, garlic, rosemary leaves, ¹/₂ teaspoon salt, 1 teaspoon pepper, the wine, and one third of the pancetta in a food processor and process until well ground. Add the remaining pancetta and pulse until just minced.

Lay the pork butt flat on a cutting board. Spread the pancetta mixture evenly over the surface of the pork. Roll the pork jelly-roll style, starting from the wider side.

Using kitchen twine, tie the rolled pork at 2-inch intervals to maintain an even shape and hold the roast together. Season with salt and pepper on all sides. Wrap in aluminum foil and refrigerate at least overnight and up to 2 days to firm up.

Preheat the oven to 240°F.

In a large roasting pan, roast the pork, still in the foil, the pan uncovered, for 3 hours. Remove from the oven, transfer to a cutting board, and let rest for 10 minutes. Remove the foil and reserve the juices.

To serve, slice the meat ¹/₂ inch thick. Divide the meat equally among the rolls. Drizzle the meat with the reserved juices and some olive oil. Close each sandwich, pressing it firmly together.

2 pounds boneless pork butt

1 tablespoon fennel seeds

4 garlic cloves, peeled

2 tablespoons fresh rosemary leaves or 1 tablespoon dried

Sea salt and freshly ground black pepper

¹/₃ cup dry red wine

8 ounces sliced pancetta, chopped

8 large crusty rolls

Extra virgin olive oil, for serving

FLORENTINE-STYLE TRIPE Tuscan cooks are famous for their homey stews that elevate humble ingredients to culinary heights. Here tripe gets transformed into incredibly tender morsels enveloped in a rich tomato sauce. If you've never had tripe before, try this simple recipe. If you already love it, we bet this will become your new favorite way to cook it. • **SERVES 6 AS AN APPETIZER OR 4 AS A MAIN COURSE**

FOR THE TRIPE

1½ pounds veal tripe

2 carrots, chopped

2 celery stalks, chopped

1 onion, chopped

3 cloves

2 bay leaves

4 fresh parsley sprigs

3 fresh thyme sprigs

½ teaspoon crushed red pepper flakes

1 teaspoon sea salt

1 teaspoon black peppercorns

FOR THE SAUCE

5 tablespoons extra virgin olive oil

½ small carrot, finely chopped

½ celery stalk, finely chopped

1 small onion, finely chopped

1 large garlic clove, minced

1 cup low-sodium chicken broth

One 24-ounce jar or can tomato puree, preferably San Marzano

Sea salt and freshly ground black pepper

6 fresh basil leaves

¾ cup fresh bread crumbs

1 cup freshly grated Parmigiano-Reggiano cheese

Put all the ingredients for the tripe in a large pot and add enough water to cover by a couple of inches. Bring to a boil and simmer, covered, until tender, about 3 hours.

Drain the tripe and set aside to cool. Discard the vegetables, herbs, and spices. Once completely cooled, pat the tripe dry with paper towels. Cut the tripe into thin strips about 2 inches long.

To make the sauce, heat 3 tablespoons of the olive oil in a large sauté pan over medium heat. Add the carrot, celery, onion, and garlic and cook until the onion is translucent and the garlic begins to color, 8 to 10 minutes. Stir in the broth, tomato puree, and tripe. Simmer for 1 hour. Season to taste with salt and pepper. The tripe can be made to this point and refrigerated, covered, for up to 3 days or frozen for 1 month. Reheat before proceeding. Remove from the heat and stir in the basil leaves.

Preheat the broiler.

Combine the bread crumbs and cheese in a small bowl. Spoon the tripe into a medium baking dish. Top with the bread-crumb mixture. Drizzle the remaining 2 tablespoons olive oil over the top and place the dish under the broiler until the top is golden, 3 to 4 minutes. Serve hot.

THE WINES OF UMBRIA

WHY UMBRIA? Why didn't we write about Tuscany? Every American's favorite spot in Italy! Even the Tuscans are trying to make Tuscany look like what Americans think it should look like: ocher walls, exposed brick, a pseudo-Etruscan vase in just the right spot. The Americans are coming; we don't want to disappoint them—they may go to Umbria.

Umbria, Tuscany the way it used to be, before Americans started buying up all those cottages under that "sun." Umbria, priced about 30 percent cheaper than Tuscany, and that includes the wines.

What the world wants from Umbria is more Orvieto. This dry (*secco*) or sweet (*amabile*) wine is made predominantly of Trebbiano grapes and is best from the Classico zone.

Our favorite Umbrian red wine is made from Sagrantino grapes in the town of Montefalco. A relatively unknown wine, Sagrantino di Montefalco has juicy red fruit flavors with a dry finish. When aged, the wine has extremely concentrated aromas of chocolate, tobacco, and vanilla. Harmonious, full-bodied, with silky tannins, even the wine in Umbria will make you forget about Tuscany.

If you really have your heart set on Tuscan wines, we recommend the wines from Isole e Olena. Paolo De Marchi, the current manager of the estate, is a fourth-generation De Marchi winemaker. Their Chianti Classico is rich and silky. They also produce a wine made with only Sangiovese grapes called Cepparello. Large-scale Tuscan wine-producing families Antinori and Frescobaldi have wine bars in Florence. There you can taste their wide range of Tuscan wines from everyday Chiantis to limited-production single-vineyard Super Tuscans, such as Tignanello and Luce.

Hurry and try these wines from Umbria before Umbria becomes the next Tuscany. But then we just heard that the Marche region is going to become the next Umbria.

O UTSIDE OF VENICE, Rome has more seafood restaurants than any other city in Italy. It was here where we first tasted *crudo,* raw seafood *all'Italiana.* The idea of dressing impeccably fresh raw seafood with great extra virgin olive oil, fresh herbs, and citrus was a revelation. Stylish and easy to prepare, crudo will give you more time away from the kitchen. Also included in this chapter are more traditional Roman-inspired family recipes and information on the crudo-friendly wines of Sicily and Sardinia.

Enoteca Cocktail

Tuna Crudo with Watercress

Yellowtail Carpaccio with Citrus and Fennel

Scallops Crudo with Lemon Thyme and Extra Virgin Olive Oil

> **Maine Shrimp Tartufato**

Black Bass Crudo with Pistachios and Pistachio Oil

Crispy Toma Cheese with Lemon Marmalade and Grilled Eggplant

Rice Balls Stuffed with Lamb, Spinach, and Cheese

Ricotta Cheese and Prosciutto Crostini

Pasta with Spinach, Pecorino Romano, and Black Pepper

Pane Fratau

Limoncello Granita

The Wines of Sicily and Sardinia

ENOTECA COCKTAIL When it's summer in Rome and it's too hot to think—too hot for even a glass of wine—we crave this refreshing cocktail that revives us and wakes up our palates.

For this special cocktail, we love Blood Orange Vodka from Charbay in California, which uses blood oranges in the distillation process, making it uniquely flavorful. If you can't find it, substitute any orange-flavored vodka.

Aperol is a delicious orange liqueur from Italy that is not widely known in America. Cocktails that use Aperol are even more obscure but have great names like the Love Me Tender, which is made with Aperol, gin, sherry, peach vodka, and apricot brandy. If that sounds a little too sweet, try the Shaft—Aperol, gin, and sparkling white wine—or the 86, Cointreau, Aperol, and vermouth. • **MAKES 1 COCKTAIL**

Shake the vodka, Aperol, and sour mix in a cocktail shaker with ice. Strain into a martini glass, garnish with an orange twist, and serve.

1½ ounces blood orange vodka

½ ounce Aperol or Campari

1 ounce sour mix

Orange twist, for garnish

TUNA CRUDO WITH WATERCRESS *Colatura di alici* is produced on the Amalfi coast in southern Italy and dates back to Roman times, when it was called *garum*. A fish sauce of anchovy extract and salt, it replaces soy as the condiment for raw fish. See the Resource Guide (page 194) for where to find colatura. Strong on its own, it mellows when paired with peppery watercress and rich raw tuna.

When buying tuna, look for bright red flesh that glistens. Avoid any dull or brown-looking meat. • **SERVES 4 AS A TASTING PORTION OR 2 AS AN APPETIZER**

Arrange the tuna on plates. Drizzle with the colatura oil and then top with the watercress. (If using olive oil, sprinkle the tuna with salt.) Drizzle the watercress with olive oil and serve.

8 ounces sushi-quality tuna, thinly sliced

1 teaspoon colatura oil or extra virgin olive oil plus sea salt

Large handful of watercress, stems removed

Extra virgin olive oil, for drizzling

YELLOWTAIL CARPACCIO WITH CITRUS AND FENNEL

Vittore Carpaccio was an Italian Renaissance painter from Venice who favored the color red. Years later, a thinly sliced raw beef presentation named after the painter became widely popular, and everybody started naming anything thin and raw *carpaccio*.

In this recipe, thinly sliced buttery yellowtail is embellished by crunchy fennel, sweet and tart orange, and a sprinkling of coriander seeds, lime zest, and a little crushed red pepper for extra kick. • **SERVES 4 AS A TASTING PORTION OR 2 AS AN APPETIZER**

1 small orange

12 ounces sushi-quality yellowtail, cut into 8 equal slices

1/2 fennel bulb, shaved or thinly sliced

2 teaspoons extra virgin olive oil

1/4 teaspoon grated lime zest

1/2 teaspoon crushed coriander seeds

Sea salt

Pinch of crushed red pepper flakes

Cut the top and bottom off the orange, exposing the flesh. Stand the orange on one end and, following the curve of the fruit, slice away the peel and a little flesh. Pick up the orange in one hand and, with a paring knife in the other, working over a bowl, slice between the membranes to release the orange segments. Squeeze the membrane to release any juice and then discard the membrane.

Lay the yellowtail on plates. Arrange the fennel and orange segments over the carpaccio. Drizzle with the oil and the orange juice. Sprinkle with the lime zest, coriander seeds, salt, and crushed red pepper flakes and serve.

SCALLOPS CRUDO WITH LEMON THYME AND EXTRA VIRGIN OLIVE OIL

Crudo is one of the simplest dishes to prepare at home, assuming you have a reliable source for sushi-quality fish and shellfish, a term used by seafood vendors to describe the freshest of the fresh. And with the ease of internet ordering, almost all of us can have beautiful fish delivered to our door. (See the Resource Guide, page 194.) While this freshness comes at a price, you will be rewarded by superior flavor reminiscent of that of the finest crudo bars in the Mediterranean.

Bay scallops are prized for their delicate and sweet flavor. East Coast bay scallops are generally available in October and November. Bay scallops from other parts of the country or the world are available all year. • SERVES 4 AS A TASTING PORTION OR 2 AS AN APPETIZER

8 ounces bay scallops

½ teaspoon fresh lemon thyme leaves

1½ tablespoons extra virgin olive oil

Scant ⅛ teaspoon salt

Combine the scallops, thyme, oil, and salt in a bowl. Spoon onto plates and serve immediately.

MAINE SHRIMP TARTUFATO

Tiny Maine shrimp are in season briefly in winter. When available, they are great served raw with black truffles. Substitute Maine shrimp for the bay scallops and 2 tablespoons chopped black truffle, fresh or jarred, for the lemon thyme.

BLACK BASS CRUDO WITH PISTACHIOS AND PISTACHIO

OIL The only place in Italy that produces pistachios is Sicily. In the town of Bronte you will find the best pistachios in all of Europe growing in the rich volcanic soil surrounding Mount Etna. The whole town is pistachio crazy. There is even a Sagra del Pistacchio, where the following preparation would undoubtedly meet much favor. If you decide to go to Bronte for the festival, be sure to go in an odd year. Pistachio trees bear fruit only every two years.

The crunchiness and flavor of chopped pistachios is intensified by the addition of pistachio oil, a great match for the mildly flavored black bass. Spigola and branzino are two types of European bass found in most Roman crudo bars. Black bass is more readily available in the United States and is very similar in taste and texture to its European cousins.

If you don't have a ring mold, a small tuna can opened at both ends to make a ring is a fine substitute. Alternatively, mound the fish on plates and top with the pistachios; the results will be every bit as delicious. See photograph on page 58. • **SERVES 6 AS A TASTING PORTION OR 4 AS AN APPETIZER**

Combine the bass with the pistachio oil, paprika, and salt in a bowl. Mix well.

Lightly oil a ring mold 2 inches tall and 2 inches wide and place in the center of one of 4 plates. Spoon in one fourth of the bass mixture, then top with 1 tablespoon of the chopped pistachios. Push down gently to pack the layers. Carefully remove the ring mold, keeping the layers intact. Drizzle with additional pistachio oil and serve. Repeat to make the remaining 3 servings.

6 ounces black bass fillet, finely diced

3 tablespoons pistachio oil, plus more for drizzling

Scant 1/8 teaspoon hot paprika

1/4 teaspoon sea salt

1/4 cup finely chopped pistachios

CRISPY TOMA CHEESE WITH LEMON MARMALADE AND GRILLED EGGPLANT
This dish is sweet, tangy, and smoky all at once. Toma cheese dates back to Roman times and is a semihard cow's milk cheese from Italy. Fresh and sweet when young, the cheese can mature for up to 12 months, becoming sharp and tangy with age. The cheese is sold in small individual molds when fresh and also made in larger molds for aging. Substitute smaller fresh-rind goat or Brie cheese rounds for the individual tomas.

The lemon marmalade and the eggplant can be made ahead, so the final assembly can be quick and easy, making this a perfect dish for guests or a light meal. Serve with a crisp white wine or a deep fruity red like Zinfandel. • **SERVES 6 AS AN APPETIZER OR 3 AS A MAIN COURSE**

FOR THE LEMON MARMALADE

2 medium lemons

1/3 cup sugar

FOR THE EGGPLANT AND CHEESE

3 Japanese eggplants

1/2 cup extra virgin olive oil, plus more for drizzling

Sea salt and freshly ground black pepper

1/2 cup all-purpose flour

2 large eggs, beaten

1/2 cup whole milk

1 cup fresh bread crumbs

6 individual fresh Toma cheeses, approximately 2 ounces each, or 12 ounces Toma cheese, cut into 6 slices

Large handful of arugula, for garnish

To make the marmalade, cut the top and bottom off the lemons, exposing the flesh. Stand each lemon on one end and, following the curve of the fruit, slice away the peel and a little flesh. Pick up the lemon in one hand and, with a paring knife in the other, working over a bowl, slice between the membranes to release the lemon segments. Squeeze the membrane to release any juice and then discard the membrane. Cut the peel (it will have the pith and some flesh attached) into long strips, about 1/4 inch wide.

Bring the peel to a boil in just enough cold water to cover in a small saucepan over medium-high heat. Drain and repeat the process twice. Combine the boiled peel, sugar, and 1/2 cup water in the saucepan and cook over medium-low heat until soft and sweet, 30 to 45 minutes.

Add the lemon segments and their juice to the mixture. Transfer the marmalade to a nonreactive bowl and refrigerate for at least 1 hour and up to 1 week before using.

Prepare a fire in a charcoal grill or preheat a gas grill to medium-high.

Place the eggplants on the grill and roast until charred and black on all sides, 10 to 15 minutes. Transfer the charred eggplants to a bowl and cover with plastic wrap. Allow the eggplants to steam for 15 minutes, then cut the eggplants in half lengthwise and scoop the flesh into a bowl. The eggplant will be very soft and pulpy. Discard the skins. Add $1/4$ cup of the olive oil to the eggplant and season with salt and pepper to taste. Set aside until ready to serve (up to 1 hour) or refrigerate for up to 3 days. Bring to room temperature before serving.

Put the flour in a bowl, whisk the eggs and milk together in a second bowl, and put the bread crumbs in a third bowl. Take a piece of cheese and dip it first in the flour, shaking off any excess. Then dip the cheese in the egg mixture, draining off any excess. Finally, coat the cheese in bread crumbs. Repeat with the remaining pieces of cheese. Refrigerate on a plate for 15 minutes.

Heat a large sauté pan over medium-high heat. Add the remaining $1/4$ cup olive oil and, when hot, add the breaded cheese and cook until golden brown on the bottom, about 1 minute. Turn the cheese over and cook for an additional minute to brown the other side. Transfer to paper towels to drain.

Place a piece of cheese on each of 6 individual plates. Spoon some of the eggplant puree and a teaspoon of lemon marmalade onto each plate next to the cheese. Drizzle with extra virgin olive oil and garnish with arugula. Serve immediately.

RICE BALLS STUFFED WITH LAMB, SPINACH, AND CHEESE

In Italy these addictive rice balls are called *arancini* because with their size and shape and golden brown color they resemble little oranges. While they were originally Sicilian, we give them a Roman twist by adding lamb, a traditional Roman ingredient.

These make delicious cocktail party or pre-dinner food, and they can be made in advance, frozen, and then cooked as needed. • **SERVES 6**

Combine the rice with 1 quart of water in a medium saucepan. Season lightly with salt and simmer over medium heat until all the water is absorbed, 10 to 15 minutes.

Pour the rice onto a cookie sheet and spread it out to cool.

Heat the olive oil in a medium sauté pan over medium heat. Add the lamb and cook for 2 minutes. Add the garlic and continue cooking until the lamb is completely browned, about 5 minutes. Add the spinach and cook until wilted, a minute or two. Remove from the heat and set aside to cool. Season with salt and pepper to taste.

When the rice is cool, stir in 2 of the eggs and 1 cup of the grated pecorino cheese. Using your hands, shape the rice into balls about 2 inches in diameter. Use your finger to make a hole and fill it with a little of the ground lamb mixture and 2 or 3 cubes of the mozzarella. Press the rice up and over the opening to close. Refrigerate for at least 30 minutes before breading.

Beat the remaining 3 eggs with a pinch of salt in a shallow bowl. Put the bread crumbs and remaining 1/2 cup pecorino in another shallow bowl. Put the flour in a third bowl. Dip the rice balls in the flour, then in the beaten eggs, and then in the bread-crumb mixture. Shake off any excess. The rice balls can be cooked immediately or refrigerated overnight or frozen for up to 1 month.

To fry, heat the canola oil in a deep-fryer or heavy-bottomed pot to 325°F.

Add half of the rice balls to the hot oil and fry, turning as needed so they brown evenly, until golden brown, about 7 minutes. Remove from the hot oil and drain on paper towels. Wait for the oil to return to 325°F before repeating with the rest of the rice balls. When cool enough to handle, after about 3 minutes, transfer to a serving plate and serve immediately.

2 cups Arborio rice

Sea salt and freshly ground black pepper

2 tablespoons extra virgin olive oil

6 ounces ground lamb

1 garlic clove, minced

Large handful of fresh spinach, stems removed

5 large eggs

1 1/2 cups grated aged Pecorino Romano, plus more for serving

1 1/2 ounces mozzarella cheese, cut into 1/4-inch dice (2 tablespoons)

1 cup dried bread crumbs, preferably panko

1/2 cup all-purpose flour

1 quart canola oil

RICOTTA CHEESE AND PROSCIUTTO CROSTINI

Ricotta is Italian for "recooked." Believed to have originated in the Roman countryside, this fresh cheese is made from the whey of cow's or sheep's milk that's drained off in the production of mozzarella, provolone, and other cheeses. Many people are already familiar with ricotta, having enjoyed it in a variety of sweet and savory dishes including lasagne, ravioli, and cannoli.

Paired with the slightly salty and faintly sweet famous Italian ham, prosciutto, this dish is one of the best ways to appreciate ricotta's creamy texture. • **SERVES 8 AS AN APPETIZER**

One 16-ounce container (2 cups) whole-milk ricotta cheese

Eight 1-inch-thick slices ciabatta bread, halved

¹/₃ cup extra virgin olive oil

Sea salt and freshly ground black pepper

16 thin slices prosciutto di Parma

Spread 2 tablespoons of ricotta cheese on each half slice of ciabatta and set on a serving platter. Drizzle the olive oil over the ricotta and season with salt and pepper. Gently fold a slice of prosciutto on top of the ricotta.

PASTA WITH SPINACH, PECORINO ROMANO, AND BLACK PEPPER

Pecorino Romano is the name of the aged grating cheese that comes from the milk of sheep that graze on the hills surrounding Rome. Its distinctive, naturally salty flavor is what makes this simple dish so satisfying.

For variety, substitute escarole, broccoli, or green beans for the spinach. • **SERVES 6 AS AN APPETIZER OR 4 AS A MAIN COURSE**

Heat the olive oil in a medium pot over medium heat. Add the garlic and cook until browned on all sides, 3 to 4 minutes. Add the spinach and cover with a tight-fitting lid. Cook until wilted, 4 to 5 minutes. Turn off the heat and leave covered on the stove.

Meanwhile, bring a large pot of salted water to a boil. Add the pasta to the pot and cook, stirring frequently, until the pasta is al dente, about 2 minutes less than what is recommended on the box. Before draining, remove 1 cup of the pasta water. Drain the pasta and transfer to a large bowl.

Add the reserved pasta water to the spinach, stirring to loosen and separate the leaves. Discard the garlic.

Add the spinach and 1 1/2 cups of the grated cheese to the pasta and season generously with pepper. Toss well to combine and allow the pasta to absorb some of the sauce.

Transfer the pasta to a platter. Top with the remaining 1 cup cheese and more freshly ground pepper. Serve immediately.

3 tablespoons extra virgin olive oil

4 garlic cloves, smashed and peeled

10 ounces fresh spinach, stems removed

1 pound linguine or spaghetti

2 1/2 cups freshly grated Pecorino Romano cheese

Freshly ground black pepper

PANE FRATAU This is our interpretation of a traditional dish found all over Sardinia, but especially in the hills away from the coasts. By adding water or milk to soften the *carta di musica,* a thin cracker-style bread, and topping it with fresh cheese, shepherds nourish themselves as they move their flocks across the rugged mountainous terrain.

If you can't find carta di musica in your local grocery store, lavash or any other cracker bread makes a fine substitute. Fiore Sardo or Pecorino Sardo is sheep's milk cheese from Sardinia that is slightly smoky in flavor. Pecorino Romano cheese can be substituted. • **SERVES 8 AS AN APPETIZER**

2 tablespoons extra virgin olive oil, plus more for drizzling

1/2 small onion, chopped

1 garlic clove, smashed and peeled

One 24-ounce jar or can tomato puree, preferably San Marzano

Sea salt and freshly ground black pepper

6 fresh basil leaves

8 pieces carta di musica, lavash, or other cracker bread

2 1/2 cups freshly grated Fiore Sardo or Pecorino Romano cheese

8 large eggs

Heat the olive oil in a medium saucepan over medium heat. Add the onion and garlic and cook until the onion is translucent and the garlic golden brown, 5 minutes. Add the tomato puree and cook for 5 minutes. Season with salt and pepper to taste. Stir in the basil leaves and keep warm.

Preheat the oven to 325°F.

Meanwhile, bring a large pot of water to a boil and then turn off the heat.

Ladle 1/3 cup of the tomato sauce into a 2-quart baking dish and set aside.

One at a time, drop a cracker-bread sheet into the water, making sure to submerge it fully without breaking it. After 1 minute, use 2 slotted spoons—one in each hand—to carefully remove the cracker bread from the water. Drain as much water as you can from the cracker and place it in the baking dish, trimming it if necessary to fit. Add another 1/3 cup of the sauce, spreading it over the cracker bread, and sprinkle with 2 tablespoons of the grated cheese.

Repeat this process, moistening the remaining cracker-bread sheets and topping each with sauce and cheese, to make a layered casserole. Top the dish with a drizzle of olive oil. Bake in the oven until set, about 20 minutes.

Meanwhile, fill a large saucepan with 2 inches of water. Bring the water to a soft boil over medium-high heat.

Remove the pane fratau from the oven and divide among 8 warm plates.

Crack 4 of the eggs, one at a time, into the boiling water and poach for 2 minutes for runny yolks, 3 minutes for medium-firm yolks. Remove the eggs with a slotted spoon, placing one on each serving. Repeat this procedure with the remaining 4 eggs.

Drizzle each serving with some olive oil, sprinkle with 1 tablespoon grated cheese, and serve immediately.

LIMONCELLO GRANITA   Granita is the original Italian ice. It is simple to make and requires no special equipment or effort other than an occasional stirring or grating to produce the right consistency.

Made from lemon peels, sugar, and alcohol (usually vodka), limoncello can be enjoyed as a *digestivo* after a meal, poured over strawberries for a delicious dessert, or mixed with sparkling wine or Prosecco as a cocktail. (See our Limoncello Martini recipe, page 81.) It is made in the towns of Sorrento, Amalfi, and Capri, south of Rome on the Amalfi coast. Each town has its own story of how it originated, but they all agree that limoncello should be served very cold. We think it's the perfect addition to this refreshing granita. • **SERVES 4**

3 lemons

1/3 cup sugar

2 tablespoons limoncello

Lemon Marmalade (page 66)

With a vegetable peeler or sharp knife, remove the zest from the lemons. Cut the peel into long, thin strips, about 1/4 inch wide. Juice the lemons to make 1/2 cup of juice.

Heat 1 cup water with the sugar in a small heavy-bottomed saucepan over medium-high heat, stirring until the sugar is dissolved. Stir in the lemon zest and let simmer for 30 seconds. Remove from the heat and stir in the limoncello and lemon juice. Set aside and cool to room temperature, about 30 minutes. Cover and chill the syrup until cold, about 1 hour.

To freeze, strain the mixture into a nonreactive loaf pan and transfer to the freezer. (Discard the zest.) Scrape the mixture with a fork every 30 minutes until the liquid becomes granular, but remains slightly slushy, 3 to 4 hours. Frozen, it will keep for 2 to 3 days.

To serve, spoon some of the marmalade into cups or small dishes. Spoon the granita on top.

THE WINES OF SICILY AND SARDINIA

HISTORICALLY AND CURRENTLY, ROME IS LINKED TO WHITE WINE.
The easy, everyday wines of the area, Frascati and Marino, are made to drink young and not travel far. These wines seem to taste best when dining alfresco in a local trattoria overlooking the Roman countryside.

Rome is also the gateway to southern Italy. Today a revolution in the vineyards, along with modern winemaking practices, has poised Italy's southern wine-producing regions for success. Thanks to the Romans for recognizing the wine-growing potential of Italy's *mezzogiorno,* where ancient grape types are still being grown today.

Two of the most exciting wine-producing regions of southern Italy are Sicily and Sardinia. Major wineries from all over Italy are investing here; for example, Giacomo Tachis, the winemaker from Sassicaia, oversees the Santadi winery in Sardinia. The climate of these sun-drenched islands provides consistent quality year after year for first-rate wines at sensible prices.

Sicily is Italy's second-largest wine-producing region, and its proudest traditional wine, Marsala, is a sweet, fortified wine that is used in cooking and for making some of Sicily's most famous desserts.

However, Sicily also makes some delicious white and red wines to accompany savory dishes. With the emphasis on quality rather than quantity, this rich-volcanic-soiled island has one of the most progressive wine industries in Italy and produces wines that are light and fruity yet full of character.

For an easy-drinking, food-friendly white, look for Etna Bianco. Made from the native Carricante grape, it is straw colored and fresh with a dry finish. Other native grapes traditionally used in making Marsala that are increasingly being made into table wines are Inzolia and Grillo. Blended together or with international varieties like Sauvignon Blanc and Chardonnay, these are refreshing, citrus-scented wines to ask for when talking to the wine merchant at your favorite wine shop.

Some of Sicily's finest reds come from the grape Nero d'Avola. Known for their black currant fruit flavors and aging ability, these wines are great food companions. A longtime staple on Italian-American restaurant wine lists, well-known Sicilian producers of Corvo and Regaleali wines continue to make wines of distinction. Prominent international varieties such as Cabernet Sauvignon, Merlot, and Syrah are showing real promise in Sicily as single-varietal bottlings or in blends with indigenous grape types. Look for wines from Planeta, Santa Anastasia, Calatrasi, Tasca d'Almerita, Ajello, Duca di Salaparuta, and Cantine EGROS.

Isolation in the middle of the Mediterranean has made Sardinia Italy's most atypical wine region. Influences from many foreigners, the Spaniards in particular, have given the wines and cuisine of Sardinia their own distinctive character.

Three producers that we have found to make consistent and delicious wines are Argiolas, Santadi, and Sella and Mosca. Their wines are excellent values and have been exported to the United States for several years.

Over the years these wineries have strongly insisted on making wine from native Sardinian grapes, the whites from Nuragus and Vermentino and the reds from Cannonau, Monica, and Carignano.

The white wines are light and quite crisp, perfect with lobster and other crustaceans. The dry reds based on Cannonau, a relative of the Garnacha grape brought to the island from Spain, have a creamy texture with hints of almond undertones and are terrific with all kinds of food, from *salumi* and nuts to roasted meats and cheeses.

There is a lot to look forward to from Sicily and Sardinia. Their quality wine production is growing, and thanks to international interest, these wines will only become more readily available.

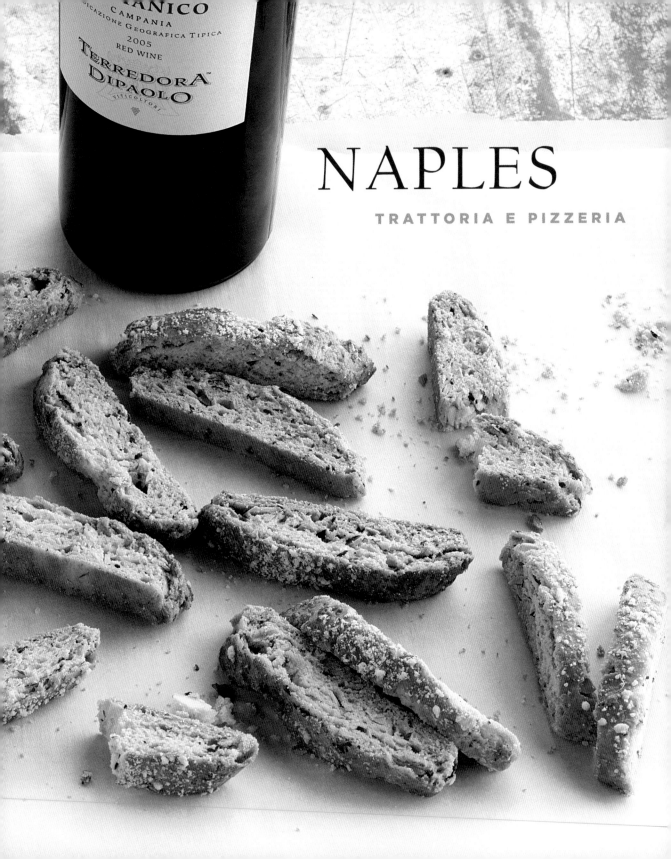

NAPLES

TRATTORIA E PIZZERIA

I N THIS CHAPTER we revel in the glory that is pizza. Pizza was born in Naples. Based on our recipe for a classic crisp and chewy crust, and topped with pleasing combinations, pizza can be the perfect anytime food. We also introduce a fun, exciting entertaining idea, the Mozzarella Bar.

Other recipes include lusty southern Italian dishes just like Nonna used to make. Highlighted are the robust and flavorful wines of Campania and Italy's southern regions.

Limoncello Martini

Mediterranean Iced Tea

Mozzarella Bar

Savory Rosemary and Parmigiano Biscotti

Potato, Garlic, and Rosemary Pizza

Double-Decker Mushroom Pizza

> **Double-Decker Sausage and Pepper Pizza**

> **Double-Decker Spinach and Tomato Pizza**

Crispy Tomato Flatbread

Pork Ribs with Garlic, Chilies, and Tomato

Neapolitan Baked Swordfish

Nonna's Broccoli Rabe

Honey Fritters

The Wines of Campania and Southern Italy

LIMONCELLO MARTINI Amalfi in southern Italy is full of lemon trees that produce the biggest, most flavorful lemons in the world. So what do you do when life hands you these lemons? Make limoncello martinis, wonderfully refreshing in spring and summer, bracing in fall and winter. • **MAKES 1 COCKTAIL**

Rub the rim of a martini glass with the lemon wedge. Put some confectioners' sugar on a small dish, tap the dish to level the sugar and invert the glass into the sugar to coat the rim.

Shake the vodka, lemon juice, and limoncello with ice in a cocktail shaker. Strain into the prepared glass and garnish with a lemon twist.

1 lemon wedge

Confectioners' sugar

1 1/2 ounces citrus-flavored vodka

1 ounce fresh lemon juice

1 ounce limoncello

Twist of lemon peel

MEDITERRANEAN ICED TEA We first tasted this drink in a bar in Naples, and we think it is the quintessential drink of Neapolitan ingenuity. Where else would they invent a drink that looks like iced tea but contains sweet orange liqueur, a splash of amaro, and the panache of southern France?

Amaro is a concentrated liqueur that can be made from herbs, spices, fruit, vegetables, and flowers. Having intense aromas, brown or even mahogany colors, and lingering licorice and spice flavors on the palate, these elixirs aid in digestion but are also enjoyed over ice, mixed with soda water, or in cocktails. • **MAKES 1 COCKTAIL**

Shake the orange liqueur, amaro, lime juice, orange juice, simple syrup, and soda with ice in a cocktail shaker. Strain over ice into a highball glass. Garnish with a lavender sprig.

1 ounce orange liqueur, such as Grand Marnier, Cointreau, or Gran Torres

1 ounce Averna amaro

1 ounce fresh lime juice

1 ounce fresh orange juice

1 ounce Simple Syrup (page 147)

Splash of soda water

Fresh lavender sprig, for garnish (optional)

MOZZARELLA BAR The mozzarella bar is a showcase for the fabulous fresh buffalo and cow's milk cheeses of southern Italy. The concept comes from Rome, where the first restaurant devoted entirely to showcasing these cheeses recently opened. Easy and fun to do, it involves nothing more than picking up some mozzarella cheeses and condiments that you want to taste and creating a self-serve appetizer bar.

Condiments of extra virgin olive oil, balsamic vinegar, sea salt, and black pepper are really all you need, though additional ones such as salumi or anchovies, as well as cherry tomatoes, grilled eggplant (page 66), marinated olives (page 3), roasted tomato (page 7), roasted peppers, fresh basil, pesto (page 27), and arugula or mixed lettuces are always welcome.

Traditionally, fresh mozzarella is shaped into rounds and ovals. Other forms of mozzarella like bocconcini, small balls, offer variety. Supplement those shapes with some fresh burrata, a buttery, creamy cheese from Apulia; see the Resource Guide (page 194).

For the mozzarella bar, we recommend finding 2 or 3 types of cheese. The idea here is to try a little of each cheese with a different condiment. Plan on about 2 ounces of each cheese per person and pick 5 or 6 accompaniments from the preceding list, in addition to a selection of extra virgin olive oils and vinegars. Here is a "recipe" for our favorite mozzarella bar. • **SERVES 4 AS AN APPETIZER**

---

8 ounces fresh mozzarella, cut into ¼-inch slices

6 ounces bocconcini (at least 12 pieces)

8 ounces burrata or fiore di latte mozzarella cheese, in 1 piece

½ cup fresh basil leaves, torn

1 cup sun-dried tomatoes

Handful of fresh arugula

1 cup Marinated Olives (page 3)

1 ounce osetra caviar (optional)

Extra virgin olive oil

Red wine vinegar

Balsamic vinegar

Sea salt and freshly ground black pepper

Put the sliced mozzarella on a plate and the bocconcini and burrata into small bowls. Put the basil, tomatoes, arugula, olives, and caviar, if serving it, into small bowls with serving utensils. Transfer the cheeses and condiments to a table or a large tray. Place the oil and vinegars, and salt and pepper around the cheeses and condiments on the mozzarella bar.

SAVORY ROSEMARY AND PARMIGIANO BISCOTTI

After a long day of observing the making of mozzarella di bufala and then tasting the incredible results, we found ourselves at a local bar in Naples to relax. The owner served us these unusual biscotti to accompany our Prosecco. Here is our interpretation, delicious with white and red wine too. See photograph on page 79. • **MAKES ABOUT 4 DOZEN BISCOTTI**

1 cup all-purpose flour, plus more for rolling

1½ teaspoons baking powder

1 tablespoon kosher salt

¼ teaspoon freshly ground black pepper

12 tablespoons (1½ sticks) unsalted butter, at room temperature

2 tablespoons sugar

3 large eggs

¼ cup freshly grated Parmigiano-Reggiano cheese, plus more for sprinkling

1 cup almonds, skin on

1 tablespoon chopped fresh rosemary leaves

Line a cookie sheet with parchment paper.

Whisk the flour, baking powder, salt, and pepper together in a medium bowl.

In the bowl of an electric mixer fitted with the paddle attachment, or by hand in a bowl with a wooden spoon, beat the butter and sugar until light and fluffy, about 5 minutes. Lightly beat the eggs in a small bowl and add to the butter bit by bit, mixing until incorporated after each addition before adding more. Add the cheese, almonds, and rosemary and mix to incorporate. Add the dry ingredients, mixing just until combined.

Divide the dough into 2 pieces, and with floured hands on a floured surface, roll each piece into a log about 14 inches long and 1 to 1½ inches in diameter. Place the logs a few inches apart on the prepared cookie sheet. Sprinkle generously with additional Parmigiano-Reggiano cheese. Refrigerate the logs for at least 30 minutes and up to overnight or freeze them for up to a month at this point. Defrost before baking.

Preheat the oven to 350°F.

Bake the logs until light brown and firm to the touch, about 30 minutes.

Remove from the oven, transfer the logs to a cutting board, and cut into ½-inch-thick slices. Arrange the slices cut side up on the baking sheet. Return to the oven for about 15 minutes, then flip and cook for another 10 minutes, or until firm. Remove from the oven and let cool completely. The biscotti will keep in an airtight container for 1 week.

POTATO, GARLIC, AND ROSEMARY PIZZA While most potato-topped pizza recipes call for sliced potatoes, we prefer to grate them. They are just as flavorful, easier to eat, and kind of remind us of hash browns. • MAKES TWO 12-INCH PIZZAS

Preheat the oven to 350°F.

While the dough is rising, bake the potatoes. Prick each potato all over with a fork. Bake until tender when pierced with a knife in the widest part, about 1 hour. Remove from the oven and transfer to a wire rack to cool. Peel the potatoes and coarsely grate them into a bowl. Set aside until ready to use.

While the potatoes are baking, cook the garlic chips. Heat the olive oil in a medium sauté pan over medium-high heat. Add the garlic and cook until golden brown, 2 to 3 minutes. Remove from the pan and set aside on paper towels to drain.

Increase the oven temperature to 500°F. Have ready 2 nonstick cookie sheets or grease 2 regular cookie sheets with olive oil.

Working with one piece of dough at a time (cover the remaining dough with a moist kitchen towel until ready to use), flatten the dough on a floured work surface. Carefully stretch the dough out with your hands. Next, gently roll out the pizza dough into a 12-inch circle about $1/8$ inch thick. Repeat with the remaining ball of dough.

Transfer the dough to the cookie sheets and brush with a thin layer of olive oil. Divide the mozzarella, grated potatoes, garlic, and rosemary between the pizzas. Season with salt and pepper. Bake the pizzas until golden brown, 12 to 15 minutes. Cut into slices and serve.

$1/2$ recipe Pizza Dough (page 86) or 1 pound store-bought refrigerated pizza dough

2 medium Yukon Gold potatoes (about $1 1/2$ pounds)

$1 1/2$ tablespoons extra virgin olive oil, plus more for brushing

2 garlic cloves, thinly sliced

1 pound fresh mozzarella cheese, shredded

Leaves from 4 fresh rosemary sprigs

Salt and freshly ground black pepper

DOUBLE-DECKER MUSHROOM PIZZA

DOUBLE-DECKER MUSHROOM PIZZA This pizza sandwich is perfect as a handheld appetizer. The double crust keeps the toppings together while adding a second layer of crunch to the pizza.

Any of your favorite pizza toppings can be substituted for the mushrooms: sausage and peppers, spinach and tomato sauce, even pepperoni. (See the end of the recipe for variations.)

Store-bought refrigerated pizza dough can be substituted for homemade dough here; you will need 2 pounds. To bake, follow the instructions on the package. • **MAKES TWO 12-INCH DOUBLE-CRUST PIZZAS**

FOR THE PIZZA DOUGH

4 cups all-purpose flour

2 teaspoons sea salt

2 envelopes active dry yeast

1 teaspoon sugar

1¼ cups lukewarm water

FOR THE FILLING

3 tablespoons extra virgin olive oil, plus more for brushing

12 ounces fresh mushrooms, preferably wild, such as chanterelle, morel, oyster, or shiitake, brushed clean and halved or quartered if large

½ teaspoon minced garlic

1 tablespoon chopped flat-leaf parsley leaves

½ cup freshly grated Parmigiano-Reggiano cheese

2 teaspoons white truffle oil (optional)

Sea salt and freshly ground black pepper

1 pound fresh mozzarella cheese, cut into ½-inch cubes

In a stand mixer fitted with a dough hook or in a large bowl, combine the flour, salt, yeast, and sugar. Add the water to the dry ingredients and mix until the water is absorbed and a shaggy dough is formed. Turn the dough out onto a lightly floured board and knead until smooth, 2 to 3 minutes. Divide the dough into 4 equal pieces and shape each piece into a ball. Place on a floured cookie sheet and cover with plastic wrap. Let the dough rise in a warm place until doubled in size, about 2 hours, or store the dough in the refrigerator overnight. If refrigerated, let the dough come to room temperature before rolling, about 1 hour.

Meanwhile, heat the olive oil in a large sauté pan over medium-high heat. Add the mushrooms and cover for 1 minute. Turn the mushrooms over, replace the cover, and cook until the mushrooms are browned evenly, 2 to 3 minutes more. Add the garlic and parsley and cook uncovered for 1 minute more.

Remove the mushrooms from the heat and transfer to a bowl to cool. Add the Parmigiano-Reggiano and the truffle oil if using it, season with salt and pepper to taste, and mix well to combine. Set aside until needed. The mushrooms can be stored overnight in the refrigerator. No need to reheat the mushrooms before using.

Preheat the oven to 500°F.

Have ready 2 nonstick cookie sheets or grease 2 regular cookie sheets with olive oil.

Working with one piece of dough at a time (cover the remaining dough with a moist kitchen towel until ready to use), flatten the dough on a floured work surface. Carefully stretch the dough out with your hands and then gently roll it out into a 12-inch circle about 1/8 inch thick. Repeat the process with the remaining balls of dough.

Brush the pizza circles with olive oil. Using a dough docker or a fork, prick 2 of the pizza circles all over. Place 1 docked pizza circle on each of the 2 cookie sheets and bake until light brown, 8 to 10 minutes. Remove from the cookie sheets and set aside.

As soon as the cookie sheets are cool, place the remaining 2 pizza circles on them. Layer the mozzarella cheese on top, spreading the cheese to the edge. Top with the mushroom mixture.

Bake the mushroom pizzas until lightly browned, 10 to 12 minutes. Remove from the oven and place the prebaked crusts on top of each mushroom pizza, pushing down gently. Return the pizzas to the oven and bake for 2 more minutes. Remove from the oven and brush the top with olive oil.

Cut each pizza into 8 slices and serve immediately.

DOUBLE-DECKER SAUSAGE AND PEPPER PIZZA

Use 12 ounces bulk sweet or hot Italian sausage. Cook the sausage in a medium non-stick sauté pan over medium-high heat until browned, 10 to 12 minutes. Transfer to paper towels with a slotted spoon to drain. For the peppers, cut 1 green bell pepper and 1 red bell pepper into 1/2-inch pieces. In the same sauté pan, wiped clean, heat 2 table-spoons olive oil over medium heat. Add the peppers and cover. Cook, stirring once or twice, until wilted and browned, 8 to 10 minutes. Use the sausage and peppers in place of the mushrooms and follow the directions above for assembly and baking.

DOUBLE-DECKER SPINACH AND TOMATO PIZZA

Use 12 ounces stemmed spinach and 2 smashed and peeled garlic cloves. Heat 3 table-spoons extra virgin olive oil in a medium sauté pan over medium-low heat. Add the garlic and cook until browned on both sides, 4 to 5 minutes. Add the spinach and cover. Cook until the spinach is just wilted, 4 minutes. Turn off the heat and allow the spinach to steam for 1 minute. Drain the spinach and cool before putting on the pizza. For the tomato sauce, use 1 cup of your favorite jarred sauce or see the recipe on page 49. To assemble, brush the tomato sauce evenly over the dough, spreading it to the edge, and use the spinach in place of the mushrooms. Follow the directions above for baking.

CRISPY TOMATO FLATBREAD Flatbreads have become very popular. These great low-sodium alternatives to bread or crackers come in a variety of flavors and thicknesses and are addictively delicious. Flatbread is perfect to serve with soups, salads, cured meats, and cheeses.

This flatbread with the flavors of tomato, garlic, and oregano reminds us of pizza, only crunchy. We like to make our flatbreads in larger pieces because, in our big family, once the flatbread goes around the table, there may not be any left for seconds. For your family, feel free to make the flatbread any size you prefer. • **MAKES 16 LARGE PIECES**

Heat the olive oil in a medium sauté pan over medium-high heat. Add the garlic and cook until golden brown, 2 to 3 minutes. Remove from the pan and set aside on paper towels to drain.

Preheat the oven to 425°F.

Transfer the rolled dough to 2 nonstick cookie sheets or regular cookie sheets greased with olive oil, so that 2 pieces will fit on each sheet. The pieces should each be approximately 4 inches wide and 12 inches long.

Brush each piece lightly with olive oil and a few tablespoons of tomato puree. Sprinkle with some oregano, salt, pepper, and garlic chips and bake until golden brown, 12 to 14 minutes. Remove from the cookie sheets and let cool completely before serving.

3 tablespoons extra virgin olive oil, plus more for brushing

4 garlic cloves, thinly sliced

Crispy Parmigiano Flatbread dough (page 20), rolled but not sprinkled with cheese

1 cup jarred or canned tomato puree, preferably San Marzano

1 tablespoon dried oregano

Sea salt and freshly ground black pepper

PORK RIBS WITH GARLIC, CHILIES, AND TOMATO These

ribs will make you forget about barbecue sauce. This recipe is based on the flavors and aromas of Sunday dinners at Grandma Mantuano's house, where the chili pepper was king and pork not far behind. For this dish we like thick and meaty country-style ribs best, but baby back ribs also work well. • SERVES 8 AS A MAIN COURSE

¼ cup extra virgin olive oil

4 pounds country-style ribs

Sea salt and freshly ground black pepper

8 garlic cloves, smashed and peeled

Two 24-ounce jars or cans tomato puree, preferably San Marzano

½ cup pickled chilies, such as spicy red cherry peppers

Preheat the oven to 325°F.

Heat a large roasting pan on top of the stove over medium heat. Add the olive oil and heat for 1 minute. Meanwhile, season the ribs with salt and pepper. Add the ribs to the pan and brown on all sides, 8 to 10 minutes. Add the garlic and brown for a minute or two. Remove the ribs and garlic from the pan and transfer to a large plate for a moment. Drain excess fat from the pan before returning the ribs and garlic to the pan. Add the tomato puree and enough water just to cover the ribs.

Transfer to the oven and braise until the meat is tender, 2½ hours. Add the chilies and cook for 30 minutes. The ribs can be refrigerated in the sauce for up to 3 days. Reheat before serving.

Transfer the ribs to a warmed platter. Ladle the sauce and chilies over the ribs and serve.

NEAPOLITAN BAKED SWORDFISH The best swordfish in Italy comes from the Straits of Messina, just south of Naples. There it is served grilled with lemon and capers, thinly sliced like carpaccio and marinated, or baked. Braising with peppers and onions mellows the fish and brings out its natural sweetness.

Swordfish has firm, flavorful meat that makes it an ideal fish for a wide range of dishes. It is best enjoyed when cut into steaks or into chunks and skewered. • **SERVES 6 AS A MAIN COURSE**

Six 5-ounce swordfish steaks

Sea salt and freshly ground black pepper

3 tablespoons extra virgin olive oil

3 garlic cloves, thinly sliced

1 red bell pepper, cut into chunks

1 green bell pepper, cut into chunks

1 small onion, cut into chunks

1/2 cup dry white wine

One 28-ounce can plum tomatoes, preferably San Marzano

1 1/2 teaspoons capers, rinsed

2 cups low-sodium chicken broth

Season the swordfish with salt and pepper. Heat the oil in a large ovenproof sauté pan over medium-high heat. Add the swordfish steaks to the pan and cook until browned on the bottom, about 3 minutes. Flip the fish over and brown the other side, about 2 minutes. Transfer the fish to a plate and set aside.

Add the garlic to the same pan and cook until lightly browned, 2 minutes. Add the bell peppers and onion and cook until slightly softened, 8 minutes. Add the wine and stir, scraping up the bits from the bottom of the pan. Cook until the wine has reduced by half, about 4 minutes. Add the tomatoes, crushing them with the side of a wooden spoon. Add the capers and the broth and then add the swordfish back to the pan. Bring to a simmer, lower the heat to maintain the simmer, and cook for 10 minutes. Season with salt and pepper to taste.

Transfer the fish and the peppers to a serving platter and serve immediately.

NONNA'S BROCCOLI RABE

NONNA'S BROCCOLI RABE Tony's grandma was taught this recipe as a young bride. Handed down from her mother-in-law, it had never been written down until now. To this day, whenever the Mantuano clan plans a get-together, the first question is "Who's going to make Nonna's broccoli rabe?"

Roasting the broccoli rabe instead of boiling it accentuates the flavor. When broccoli rabe is not available, do as Grandma did: substitute a combination of Savoy cabbage and regular broccoli for a mellower version. • **SERVES 6 AS A SIDE DISH**

Preheat the oven to 375°F.

Heat the oil in a large Dutch oven or other ovenproof pot over low heat. Add the broccoli rabe and raise the heat to medium. Cook, stirring occasionally, until the broccoli rabe begins to wilt, 10 to 12 minutes. Add the cheese, bread crumbs, and allspice, season with salt and pepper, and stir well to combine.

Transfer the pot to the oven and bake until tender, 8 to 10 minutes. Remove from the oven and serve immediately.

3 tablespoons extra virgin olive oil

2 pounds broccoli rabe (rapini), cut into 1-inch pieces

1½ cups freshly grated Pecorino Romano cheese

½ cup dried bread crumbs

Scant ⅛ teaspoon ground allspice

Sea salt and freshly ground black pepper

HONEY FRITTERS The Mantuano Food Shop was a busy neighborhood grocery store serving the needs of the Italian immigrant community in Kenosha, Wisconsin. Run by Salvatore and Gisella Mantuano, Tony's grandparents, the store offered fresh meats and cheeses, dry goods, and produce. As busy as they were, especially around the holidays, Grandma still found the time to make mountains of honey-glazed fritters that the family called *scalidi*.

Every Mediterranean country has some version of "fried dough," either sprinkled with sugar or dipped in honey. Scalidi are the typical fritters of southern Italy. These fritters can be enjoyed all year and go very nicely with sweet wine.

The fritters must be made a day in advance and left to sit overnight. They are actually better the second and third day after you make them, as the honey has time to soak in.

● **MAKES ABOUT 12 FRITTERS**

12 large egg yolks

1 large egg

1 tablespoon unsalted butter, melted and cooled

1⅓ cups all-purpose flour

¼ teaspoon baking powder

1½ teaspoons sugar

2 teaspoons anise or almond extract

2 quarts canola oil for deep-frying

2 cups honey

In an electric mixer fitted with the paddle attachment, beat the egg yolks and egg on medium-high speed until thick and light in color, 15 minutes. Add the butter and beat for 1 minute. Meanwhile, in a separate bowl, whisk together the flour, baking powder, and sugar. Add half of the flour mixture and the extract to the egg mixture and mix well to combine. Add the remaining dry ingredients slowly and in small batches. Turn the dough out onto a floured board. The dough will be very sticky.

Lightly dust the dough with flour. Break off Ping Pong ball–size pieces and roll out into 10-inch strands. Pinch the ends together to form a ring. Repeat the process until all the dough is used.

To fry, heat the canola oil in a deep-fryer or heavy-bottomed pot to 335°F.

Fry the rings in the oil until golden brown, 1 to 2 minutes on each side. Drain on paper towels and let dry for 2 to 3 hours.

Heat the honey in a medium saucepan over medium-low heat until warm. While the honey heats, set a wire rack over a rimmed cookie sheet.

Spear a fritter with a fork and then dip it into the honey until well coated. Drain on the wire rack. Repeat with the remaining fritters. Once cooled, store in an airtight container at least overnight and up to 2 weeks before serving.

THE WINES OF CAMPANIA AND SOUTHERN ITALY

A GLASS OF WINE FROM CAMPANIA practically transports you to the beautiful Amalfi coast—the spectacular views, the wonderful seaside seafood restaurants, and historic Naples.

Campania is the land of archaeological grape varieties, where the grapes date back to antiquity and the wines have names like Fiano di Avellino and Greco di Tufo. Falanghina, the old grape that is now new and hot again, was the grape behind the favorite wine of Rome more than two thousand years ago. Modern winemaking techniques together with these old, lesser-known varietals are making for some of the most exciting and affordable wines from Italy. Campania is a budding major-quality region.

Sometimes called "the Barolo of the South," Taurasi, made from Aglianico grapes, is the big red here. Introduced by the Greeks, this inky, dark-colored wine has alluring bitter chocolate undertones, concentrated fruit flavors, and firm tannins that mellow with time. Aglianico pairs well with a juicy grilled steak or roast lamb.

In Apulia the leading grape is Negroamaro, or "black and bitter." The name doesn't do the wines justice. These wines are rustic, offering tar and leather on the nose and sweet spice on the palate. Try them with roasted and cured meats and full-flavored cheeses. Our personal favorite wine from the grape is called Salice Salentino, a great value for under $15 a bottle.

Another grape grown in Apulia is Primitivo, sometimes called "the father of the Zinfandel grape" (the grapes are genetically identical but not one and the same). Primitivo wines have clove and eucalyptus aromas and robust, zesty cherry and blackberry fruit flavors. These full-flavored wines are perfect with hearty dishes for cold, wintry nights.

Calabria, the region from which the Mantuano family emigrated, is not very famous for wine. That said, you should run, not walk, to your nearest wine merchant for a bottle of Gravello, a wine made from Gaglioppo and Cabernet Sauvignon grapes by our *paesani* at Librandi. Try it with Pork Ribs with Garlic, Chilies, and Tomato (page 90).

Wines from Campania and the southernmost regions of Italy are available in wine shops across the country. These are quality wines of character and flavor at affordable prices.

SEVILLE

TAPAS AND SHERRY

T HESE TAPAS bar specialties, enjoyed with a glass of sherry or other Spanish wine, suggest how the locals eat. These small-plate dishes also contain the exotic aromas and flavors of North Africa.

Falafel Crab Cakes

Saffron-Pickled Cauliflower

Pomegranate-Glazed Salmon with Mejadra

Santander Salad

Crispy Lamb Shoulder with Peas and Mint

Moroccan Vegetables

Duck Pinchos with Harissa and Sumac on Israeli Couscous

Grilled Short Ribs

Mascarpone-Filled Dates with Chocolate

Raisin Ice Cream with Pedro Ximénez Sherry

Sherry: Well Known Yet Underappreciated

FALAFEL CRAB CAKES

FALAFEL CRAB CAKES Chickpeas are a common ingredient in the cooking of southern Spain, which owes many culinary inspirations to the Moors of Northern Africa. Here we use crisp dried chickpeas to make crab cakes with an extra-crunchy crust and no bread crumbs. See photograph on page 97. • **MAKES 6 CRAB CAKES**

Soak the chickpeas in enough water to cover by several inches for 24 hours.

Drain the chickpeas well and combine in a food processor with the cilantro, scallion, jalapeño, garlic, cumin, and baking powder. Process until the mixture is well combined and the chickpeas are finely chopped; do not process into a paste.

Put the falafel mixture into a large bowl and add the crabmeat and lemon zest. Gently mix and season to taste with salt and pepper. Form the crab mixture into six 2-inch round patties, pressing the ingredients together somewhat firmly. The crab cakes can be refrigerated for up to 8 hours.

Pour ½ inch olive oil into a skillet large enough to hold all the crab cakes without touching. Heat over medium-high heat until the oil begins to smoke slightly. Add the crab cakes and cook until golden brown, 5 minutes on each side. Drain on paper towels for 2 minutes.

Serve immediately on individual plates with a dollop of tzatziki sauce on the side.

³/₄ cup dried chickpeas

½ cup (lightly packed) coarsely chopped fresh cilantro leaves

1 scallion, chopped

¼ jalapeño pepper

1 garlic clove, peeled

¼ teaspoon ground cumin

½ teaspoon baking powder

12 ounces lump blue crab meat

Grated zest of 1 lemon

Sea salt and freshly ground black pepper

1 to 2 cups extra virgin olive oil, for frying

Tzatziki Sauce (page 189)

SAFFRON-PICKLED CAULIFLOWER This bright, zesty cauliflower is very versatile and works well paired with cured meats and salads, as a side dish with Porchetta Panini (page 55), or as part of the Mozzarella Bar (page 82).

Saffron is the stigma from the crocus flower. Its distinctive red and orange strands impart a woody, earthy flavor and a beautiful golden-yellow hue to food. Widely used in cooking all over the world, as well as in familiar Mediterranean dishes such as paella, risotto Milanese, and bouillabaisse, saffron is available whole or ground, with the best coming from Spain and Greece.

For optimal flavor, purchase saffron in small amounts and store in a cool, dry place. Stored in this way, saffron will keep for at least 3 years. Because saffron is grown and harvested by hand, yielding only 3 stigmas per flower, it is considered the most expensive spice in the world. • **MAKES 4 CUPS**

2 cups white wine vinegar

2 tablespoons sea salt

1/4 cup sugar

1 small shallot, thinly sliced

5 garlic cloves, smashed and peeled

1/2 teaspoon saffron threads or 1/4 teaspoon powder

1 medium head of cauliflower, cut into florets

Freshly ground black pepper

Combine the vinegar, salt, sugar, shallot, garlic, and saffron with 2 cups water in a large saucepan. Bring to a boil over medium-high heat. Add the cauliflower florets and cook until crisp-tender, 2 minutes.

Take the pot off the heat and transfer the cauliflower with the liquid to a nonreactive container. Season with pepper and refrigerate for at least 3 hours before serving. The cauliflower can be stored in the refrigerator for up to 2 weeks.

POMEGRANATE-GLAZED SALMON WITH MEJADRA This

lacquered salmon dish is as delicious as it is beautiful. Mejadra is a dish found in the Bible and is always made with lentils and usually rice mixed together with spices and other ingredients. In this recipe, we chose a mix of garlic and ginger to add to the lentils and rice.

Purchase wild salmon if possible, as its flavor will stand up nicely to the pomegranate glaze. Pomegranate molasses is available in most Middle Eastern groceries. • **SERVES 4 AS A MAIN COURSE**

Combine the lentils with enough water to cover by 1 inch in a medium saucepan over medium-high heat. Bring to a boil and cook just until tender, about 30 minutes. Drain and set aside.

In another medium saucepan, combine the rice and saffron with 1 cup water and a pinch of salt and bring to a boil. Reduce the heat to low, cover the pot with a tight-fitting lid, and simmer until the rice is tender and nearly all of the liquid has been absorbed, 15 minutes. Remove from the heat and let stand, covered, for 5 minutes.

Heat 3 tablespoons of the oil in a medium sauté pan over medium heat. Add the garlic, ginger, and jalapeño and cook until tender, 3 to 4 minutes. Add the lentils and rice to the pan, tossing to mix the ingredients. Season to taste with salt and pepper. Keep warm while you cook the fish.

Preheat the oven to 400°F.

Heat the remaining 3 tablespoons of oil in a large oven-proof sauté pan, preferably nonstick, over high heat.

Season the fish with salt and pepper on both sides and, when the oil is hot, add it to the pan. Cook until the bottom has a toasted brown crust, 3 to 4 minutes. Turn over and brush the fillets with a generous amount of molasses. Transfer the pan to the oven and cook until the fish is opaque throughout when prodded with the tip of a knife, about 4 minutes.

Divide the lentils and rice among 4 warm plates, top each serving with a salmon fillet, and serve immediately.

½ cup dried lentils

½ cup long-grain rice

Small pinch of saffron threads

Sea salt and freshly ground black pepper

¼ cup plus 2 tablespoons extra virgin olive oil

2 tablespoons minced garlic

2 tablespoons minced peeled fresh ginger

2 tablespoons minced jalapeño pepper

Four 6-ounce skinless salmon fillets

¼ cup pomegranate molasses

SANTANDER SALAD

We have been making this simple, colorful salad of braised leeks, roasted peppers, tuna, and greens every summer since we first enjoyed it in the coastal Spanish town of Santander. Popular throughout Spain, this salad is best made with either Italian or Spanish canned tuna packed in olive oil. Even better would be to use canned tuna *ventresca,* or belly (think *toro*), from either country. • **SERVES 4 AS AN APPETIZER OR 2 AS A MAIN COURSE**

2 small leeks, split lengthwise

1 teaspoon extra virgin olive oil

Sea salt and freshly ground black pepper

Large handful of frisée or escarole hearts

2 roasted red bell peppers, sliced into strips

One 8- to 10-ounce can tuna in olive oil, preferably imported from Spain or Italy, drained

8 large green olives, such as Cerignola

8 boquerones (pickled white anchovies)

Sherry Vinaigrette (recipe follows)

Lay the leeks cut side down in a medium sauté pan and add water just to cover along with the olive oil and a pinch of salt. Simmer gently over low heat until tender, about 15 minutes. Remove from the heat and let cool in the poaching liquid. Transfer to paper towels and pat dry. Remove or trim away any outside leaves that are still tough. Discard the liquid.

To serve, place the leeks on a plate and season with salt and pepper. Top the leeks with the frisée and then the peppers. Lightly season again with salt and pepper. Top with the tuna and garnish with the olives and anchovies. Drizzle with the vinaigrette.

SHERRY VINAIGRETTE
MAKES ABOUT 2/3 CUP

2 tablespoons sherry vinegar

1 small shallot, minced

1/4 teaspoon sugar

1/8 teaspoon sea salt

1/8 teaspoon freshly ground white pepper

1/2 cup extra virgin olive oil

Combine the vinegar, shallot, sugar, salt, and white pepper in a bowl. Stir until the sugar is dissolved. In a slow stream, drizzle in the olive oil, whisking constantly until the vinaigrette is well blended. The vinaigrette can be refrigerated overnight. Whisk to recombine before serving.

CRISPY LAMB SHOULDER WITH PEAS AND MINT

Lamb shoulder is a relatively inexpensive cut of meat that becomes quite tender when cooked slowly. Cooking it a second time in a very hot oven gives you something we like to call "lamb bacon," because it's crispy on the outside. • **SERVES 8 AS AN APPETIZER OR 4 AS A MAIN COURSE**

2 pounds boneless lamb shoulder

Sea salt and freshly ground black pepper

4 garlic cloves, smashed

Grated zest of 1/2 lemon

4 fresh thyme sprigs

1 quart low-sodium chicken broth

3 tablespoons olive oil

1 tablespoon unsalted butter

1/2 sweet onion, finely chopped

1 1/2 cups fresh or thawed frozen peas

1 tablespoon torn fresh mint leaves

Preheat the oven to 250°F.

Generously season the lamb with salt and pepper. Place the lamb, garlic, lemon zest, and thyme in a Dutch oven or roasting pan just large enough to hold the lamb snugly. Add the broth to cover.

Transfer to the oven and cook until the lamb is very tender, 6 to 8 hours. Remove from the oven and let cool. The lamb can be refrigerated overnight.

Preheat the oven to 500°F.

Cut the lamb into 8 pieces.

Heat the oil over high heat in an ovenproof sauté pan just big enough to hold the lamb in a single layer. Add the lamb and cook on one side until browned lightly, 3 to 4 minutes. Turn the lamb over and transfer the pan to the oven. Cook, turning the lamb every 5 minutes or so, until the lamb crisps up evenly, about 15 minutes.

Meanwhile, melt the butter in a small saucepan over medium heat. Add the onion and a pinch of salt, cover, and cook until the onion is translucent, 12 minutes. Do not brown. Add the peas and a little pepper, cover, and cook until the peas are tender but still bright green, 3 to 5 minutes. Remove from the heat and stir in the mint leaves. Season with salt and pepper to taste.

Transfer the peas to a warm platter. Place the lamb on top of the peas and serve immediately.

MOROCCAN VEGETABLES

MOROCCAN VEGETABLES When we sailed through the Straits of Gibraltar, we were struck by how little distance separates the continents of Europe and Africa. Morocco is so close to Spain that for many it's just a day trip away.

The kaleidoscope of flavors that make up Moroccan cooking is reflected in this dish, which makes a great starter, side, or—served over couscous—vegetarian main course.

• **SERVES 6 AS A TASTING PORTION, 4 AS A SIDE DISH, OR 2 AS A MAIN COURSE**

Combine the red pepper flakes, cumin, coriander, and fennel seeds in a food processor. Pulse to chop, then add the cinnamon, salt, pepper, honey, and vinegar and process to combine. With the machine running, add the oil in a slow stream. Process until well combined.

Preheat the oven to 425°F.

Toss the eggplant, bell peppers, onion, and zucchini with the marinade in a large bowl and coat well. Transfer to a cookie sheet and roast, turning the vegetables every 5 minutes, until caramelized, 15 to 20 minutes.

Put the chickpeas into a serving bowl. Pour the hot, roasted vegetables over the beans and stir to combine.

Sprinkle with the almonds and cilantro sprigs and serve the harissa in a small bowl on the side.

3/4 teaspoon crushed red pepper flakes

1 teaspoon cumin seeds

1 teaspoon coriander seeds

1 teaspoon fennel seeds

1/4 teaspoon ground cinnamon

3/4 teaspoon sea salt

3/4 teaspoon freshly ground black pepper

1/4 cup honey

1/2 cup balsamic vinegar

3/4 cup extra virgin olive oil

1 small eggplant, cut into 1 1/2-inch pieces

1 small yellow bell pepper, cut into 1 1/2-inch pieces

1 small red bell pepper, cut into 1 1/2-inch pieces

1 small onion, cut into 1 1/2-inch pieces

2 small zucchini, cut into 1 1/2-inch pieces

One 15-ounce can chickpeas, rinsed and drained

1/2 cup sliced almonds, toasted

6 fresh cilantro sprigs

Harissa (page 107)

DUCK PINCHOS WITH HARISSA AND SUMAC ON ISRAELI COUSCOUS
These skewered mini-kebabs are found in tapas bars all over Spain. Rich duck pairs well with *harissa,* a fiery hot pepper sauce from North Africa that we tone down a bit here by using predominately red bell peppers mixed with crushed red pepper flakes.

The sumac in this recipe is not the poisonous bush found in North America that turns red in the fall, but rather a wild bush from the Mediterranean. The berries, prized for their tart citrus flavor, are dried and ground to a powder. Sumac adds a bright and delicious dimension to the duck and can be used on chicken, vegetables, and rice dishes. See the Resource Guide (page 194) for where to buy sumac.

Israeli couscous, also known as Middle Eastern couscous, is larger than traditional couscous and the superior texture rounds out this dish.

If using wood skewers, be sure to soak them in water before threading the duck onto them to prevent burning. • **SERVES 4 AS AN APPETIZER OR 2 AS A MAIN COURSE**

Cut each breast in half lengthwise and then into 4 pieces to make 32 pieces. Put in a bowl and toss with the pomegranate molasses and some salt and pepper. Put 8 pieces of duck on each of 4 skewers. Cover and refrigerate for 1 hour or overnight.

Prepare the harissa: In a blender or food processor, puree the roasted peppers with the garlic, caraway, coriander, olive oil, red pepper flakes, 1/2 teaspoon salt, and 1/4 teaspoon pepper until smooth. The harissa can be refrigerated overnight or up to 3 days.

Prepare a charcoal grill or preheat a gas grill to medium-high heat.

Prepare the couscous as directed on the package.

Grill the skewers until browned on all sides, about 8 minutes total for medium-rare. Remove from the grill, sprinkle with the sumac, and serve immediately over the couscous with the harissa on the side.

Four 4-ounce duck breasts

1/4 cup pomegranate molasses

Sea salt and freshly ground black pepper

2 roasted red bell peppers

1 garlic clove, peeled

1/8 teaspoon ground caraway

1/8 teaspoon ground coriander

2 tablespoons extra virgin olive oil

1/4 teaspoon crushed red pepper flakes

1 cup Israeli couscous

1/2 teaspoon powdered sumac

GRILLED SHORT RIBS Short ribs are usually braised slowly until tender and served as a main course. In this recipe we marinate them slowly but then grill them quickly and serve them as an appetizer. Ask your butcher to slice them thinly. You can also broil them with equally fabulous results.

This recipe embraces the historic Arab influences found in the cuisine of Seville. The combination of spices, zests, vinegar, and honey makes these ribs taste terrific, especially when paired with a glass of dry rosé. • **SERVES 4 AS AN APPETIZER**

1 cup balsamic vinegar

1 cup soy sauce

1 tablespoon honey

1 tablespoon minced peeled fresh ginger

1 tablespoon minced garlic

½ teaspoon crushed red pepper flakes

½ teaspoon dried oregano

1 teaspoon coriander seeds, toasted and crushed

1 tablespoon grated orange zest

1 tablespoon grated lemon zest

1 teaspoon sea salt

½ teaspoon freshly ground black pepper

3 pounds bone-in beef short ribs, sliced crosswise ½ inch thick

⅓ cup sesame seeds, toasted

Fresh cilantro sprigs, for garnish

In a nonreactive shallow dish just large enough to hold the ribs, combine the vinegar, soy, honey, ginger, garlic, red pepper flakes, oregano, coriander, orange and lemon zests, salt, and pepper. Add the ribs and turn to coat. Cover and marinate in the refrigerator for at least 6 hours or overnight.

Prepare a fire in a charcoal grill or preheat a gas grill to medium-high.

Drain the ribs and discard the marinade. Grill the ribs until slightly charred and crispy, about 3 minutes on each side.

Remove from the grill and transfer the ribs to a cutting board. Chop each rib into 3 or 4 pieces, between the bones. Transfer to a platter and sprinkle with the sesame seeds and cilantro sprigs. Serve immediately.

MASCARPONE-FILLED DATES WITH CHOCOLATE This simple yet satisfying sweet showcases dates, a classic Moorish ingredient. These dates can be assembled in advance and brought out shortly before serving to allow them to come to room temperature. • MAKES 12

12 fresh dates

1/2 cup mascarpone cheese

1/4 cup heavy cream, whipped

2 ounces bittersweet chocolate, grated

Cut the dates in half lengthwise on one side only, leaving them connected on the other side. Remove the pits.

In a small bowl, blend the mascarpone with the whipped cream until smooth. Place the cheese mixture into a pastry bag if desired.

Pipe or spoon the cheese mixture into each date, filling the cavity where the pit was. Press the date to close somewhat around the cheese. Roll the top of the date in the grated chocolate so it sticks to the cheese. Place on a serving plate.

Serve at cool room temperature.

RAISIN ICE CREAM WITH PEDRO XIMÉNEZ SHERRY

We first encountered this irresistible twist on rum-raisin ice cream with the owners of the highly regarded sherry firm Bodegas Hidalgo–La Gitana at a restaurant that overlooks the beautiful beaches near Sanlúcar de Barrameda. This spot, where the Guadalquivir River meets the Atlantic Ocean, we are told, is where Christopher Columbus set sail in 1492. Had he been presented this dessert made with rich, dark, sweet Pedro Ximénez sherry, he might never have left. • SERVES 8

1 cup (firmly packed) raisins

²/₃ cup Pedro Ximénez sherry, plus more for serving

3 cups heavy cream

1½ cups whole milk

8 large egg yolks

¾ cup sugar

Combine the raisins and sherry in a small nonreactive bowl. Cover and allow the raisins to sit at room temperature for 2 hours to plump. Fill a large bowl halfway with ice water and nestle a medium bowl in the ice bath.

Bring the cream and milk to a simmer in a large heavy-bottomed saucepan over medium heat. Meanwhile, whisk the egg yolks and sugar in a large bowl until pale in color. While whisking, slowly add 1 cup of the hot cream mixture. When blended, return the entire mixture to the saucepan and cook over medium-low heat, stirring constantly, until the custard thickens and coats the back of a spoon, up to 15 minutes.

Strain the custard into the medium bowl, set back in the ice bath, and let cool completely, stirring occasionally. Remove from the ice bath and add the raisins and sherry. Cover and refrigerate until cold, at least 2 hours or overnight.

Transfer the custard to an ice-cream maker and process according to the manufacturer's instructions. Transfer the ice cream to a covered container and put in the freezer until firm.

To serve, scoop ice cream into individual bowls. Top each serving with a shot of Pedro Ximénez sherry.

SHERRY: WELL KNOWN YET UNDERAPPRECIATED

JEREZ, OR SHERRY, ONE OF SPAIN'S MOST IMPORTANT WINES, is not well understood in this country. People tend to think of the wines as either thin and miserably dry or old-fashioned and cloyingly sweet. Not to taste sherry would be to deny yourself some of the world's most extraordinary wines.

Sherry is fortified wine, meaning it is higher in alcohol than everyday table wine (from 15.5 to 22 percent versus 12 to 14.5 percent) because clear brandy is added.

Sherry comes in seven styles, from the extremely dry fino to candylike sweet Pedro Ximénez. These handcrafted wines are meant to be sipped and savored, for they offer wine drinkers layers of flavor. They also come with very reasonable prices.

Because sherry goes very well with a wide variety of food, serving these wines with something to eat seems to be our best strategy to get guests to try them. Our friends usually catch on that they are not drinking just any white wine, at which point they admit that they like the wine but might not have tried it otherwise.

We start with our favorite sherry, manzanilla. It is elegant, dry, and light in color. Coming from the seaside town of Sanlúcar de Barrameda, the only place manzanilla is made, the wine gets a salty crispness from the ocean air. Fino sherry is pale and bone dry. Light and delicate fino and manzanilla both are great with appetizers such as almonds and olives, dishes of fried fish and marinated anchovies, and with shellfish prepared in every way. Both should be drunk quite chilled and kept no longer than a day or two in the refrigerator once opened.

Sherry flavors deepen as you go down the line. Amontillado is an aged fino, amber in color and nutty in flavor. Most are dry, but some are slightly sweetened. Palo cortado is a rare type of dry amontillado, sometimes described as a cross between oloroso and amontillado. Oloroso is aromatic, full-bodied, and dry. These three sherries are great wines for all kinds of cheese.

Cream sherry was originally made for the British sherry-consuming market. It is made from blending oloroso with Pedro Ximénez. Cream sherries are dark, smooth, and can be quite sweet. As far as we're concerned, we'd prefer to skip the cream sherry and just go straight to the Pedro Ximénez. If you like port or dessert wines, you will enjoy this sherry. Served at a cool room temperature, it is great for sipping on a cold winter evening or poured over ice cream. See our recipe on page 111.

We know sherry will probably never be as popular here as it is in Spain, but it has its purpose. Sherry is best served in *copitas,* wineglasses with shorter, slim stems whose bowls are narrowed at the mouth to direct the aromas. There are many excellent sherry-producer bottlings available in this country. Look for Lustau, Hidalgo, Gonzalez Byass, Sandeman, and Osborne.

THERE'S A PARTY IN THE PANTRY

YES, IT'S TRUE. We unabashedly recommend using canned and jarred foods. These are not just any products. Many of them are government-protected, best-of-a-kind ingredients now available to the home cook. Beyond olive oil, vinegar, and anchovies, these ready-to-use foodstuffs allow you to throw a party at the drop of a hat.

It is the custom in Spain to use the best canned or jarred products whenever possible, because they are of extremely high quality. We were converted to this practice one day at one of the most fabulous tapas bars in Barcelona, called Quimet & Quimet, where they astonishingly serve only jarred or canned Spanish products for all of their tapas. This place is so popular that on any given day the crowds at this tiny, popular bar spill out into the street and then enlist the rooftops of nearby parked cars as ad hoc tabletops.

Not only in Spain, but all over Europe, storing these time-saving specialties in the pantry is more than a smart way to negotiate a busy lifestyle without compromise. It is also a way of preserving the best of the best for the right moment.

Below we identify each product, suggesting how to use it. These suggestions are just a starting point. The possibilities are endless.

Let the party begin!

VEGETABLES

PASSATA DI POMODORO (Italian tomato puree with basil) • Mix with olive oil, oregano, and capers as a fresh tomato dipping sauce for bread. This is also the best tomato product for making any kind of tomato sauce. See our recipe (page 49).

MARINATED ZUCCHINI in extra virgin olive oil • Serve with ricotta cheese with some crusty bread.

ASSORTED VEGETABLE ANTIPASTO in extra virgin olive oil • This is the perfect accompaniment to an assortment of cured meats (see page 34).

DRIED TOMATOES packed in olive oil • Chop these up and serve them in salads.

PORCINI MUSHROOMS IN OLIVE OIL AND VINEGAR from Italy • Use as a garnish for fresh mozzarella and a little balsamic vinegar.

MUSHROOM SPREAD from Italy • Spread on crostini with some Brunello wine jelly.

LAMPASCIONI from Italy (grilled and marinated shallotlike bulbs of a wild hyacinth plant) • Serve with cured meats or as a vegetable antipasto; they're crunchy and smooth with a nutty taste.

DOLMAS from Greece (grape leaves stuffed with rice) • Serve as a garnish for cured meats (page 34) and cheeses (page 138).

PIQUILLO PEPPERS from Spain • These roasted peppers are great with tuna or mackerel and a drizzle of olive oil.

WHITE ASPARAGUS from Spain • Drizzle with vinaigrette or use in our White Asparagus Salad (page 132).

GARBANZO BEANS from Spain • Make a salad with these and the Spanish asparagus; drizzle with Spanish olive oil and red wine vinegar.

OLIVES from Spain • Serve with chorizo, Manchego cheese, and crusty bread.

GREEK OLIVES • Use as a garnish for Italian mackerel.

PROVENÇAL OLIVES • These are perfect with cured meats (page 34).

CAPER PESTO from Italy • Toss with warm pasta and Sicilian tuna.

CAPERS IN SALT from Italy • After rinsing, place a few of these on a cracker with some tuna and a little bergamot marmalade.

CORNICHONS from France • These are a great accompaniment for cured meats (page 34).

HARISSA SAUCE from Morocco • Try this fiery spread with Spanish garbanzo beans or use with the Duck Pinchos recipe (page 107).

SEAFOOD

MEDITERRANEAN RED TUNA IN OLIVE OIL with sea salt from Italy • Sprinkle with capers and olives.

MEDITERRANEAN TUNA "TORO" IN OLIVE OIL and sea salt from Italy • Season with oregano, a squeeze of lemon, and some freshly cracked black pepper.

SICILIAN TUNA TORO IN OLIVE OIL • Season with some sea salt that is infused with Mediterranean herbs.

SPANISH TUNA IN OLIVE OIL • Mix with Spanish garbanzo beans and herb-infused sea salt.

SMOKED TUNA from Spain • Serve with capers and piquillo peppers.

ITALIAN MACKEREL IN OLIVE OIL with sea salt • Garnish with olives and capers.

MEDITERRANEAN SARDINES IN OLIVE OIL • Combine with marinated zucchini or vinaigrette and serve on toasted bread for an excellent tapa.

ANCHOVIES from Spain • Wrap around a hard-cooked quail egg and a piquillo pepper and spear with a toothpick.

COLATURA (ANCHOVY ESSENCE) from Italy • This sauce is delicious as a seasoning for crudo (pages 64–65).

ACCOMPANIMENTS FOR CURED MEATS AND CHEESE

HANDCRAFTED BREADSTICKS with extra virgin olive oil from Italy • Serve with assorted salumi or prosciutto.

OLIVE OIL CRACKERS from Spain • These make a nice partner for cheese and honey.

SARDINIAN CARTA DI MUSICA • A thin crackerlike bread, this is great topped with ricotta, corbezzolo honey, and prosciutto. Use in the Pane Fratau recipe (page 72).

FIG CAKE from Spain • Use as a condiment for any blue cheese.

ITALIAN FIGS • Serve together with some chorizo and manchego cheese.

ZIBIBBO GRAPE GELATINA from Pantelleria, Sicily • Serve with cheese or any paté.

RED WINE JELLY from Italy • Use as a garnish for cured meats or hard cheeses.

BRUNELLO WINE JELLY from Italy • Serve with salami.

CORBEZZOLO HONEY from Sardinia • Something like a honeyed caramel sauce, with a unique flavor on its own, this honey is wonderful drizzled over ricotta or mascarpone cheese.

BARCELONA

MODERN SPANISH WINE BAR

ONE OF OUR FAVORITE CITIES, Barcelona amazes us with its great architecture and the staggering La Boqueria market. A few hours spent exploring the stalls should include lunch at one of the many family-owned tapas bars there. Small plates of food prepared before your eyes create quite an appetite. The dishes we enjoyed there, all washed down with Cava, Spain's sparkling wine, inspired us to re-create the experience here for you.

Tomato Bread with Serrano Ham and Manchego Cheese

Mediterranean Spiced Nuts

Warm Octopus with Potatoes and Smoked Paprika

Charred Baby Leeks with Romesco Sauce

Catalonian Pizza

Razor Clams a la Plancha

Fried Eggs with Mushrooms, Garlic, and Parsley

White Asparagus Salad

Garlic Shrimp with Chilies and Rosemary

Carajillo

Cava and the Wines of Northern Spain

TOMATO BREAD WITH SERRANO HAM AND MANCHEGO CHEESE

A tapas bar staple, this dish is easy to make and always pleases, provided you follow four simple points: Make this dish only when tomatoes are great. Use quality manchego cheese, preferably aged for six months. Drizzle with excellent olive oil. Finally, use only imported Serrano ham, thinly sliced. Although the bread is important, if you adhere to those four points, it may be enough to make even presliced sandwich bread taste great (not that we are suggesting that). • **MAKES 6 PIECES**

Cut the tomatoes in half and rub the cut side of one half against one slice of bread, pressing firmly until the juice of the tomato soaks into the bread. Repeat with the remaining tomato halves and bread slices. Discard the tomatoes. Top each piece of tomato bread with cheese and then ham. Drizzle each piece with olive oil and serve.

3 ripe plum tomatoes

Six 1-inch slices baguette

6 thin slices manchego cheese, about the same size as the bread

6 thin slices Serrano ham

Extra virgin olive oil, for drizzling

MEDITERRANEAN SPICED NUTS
This easy-to-make, do-ahead recipe turns dried chickpeas, fava beans, and almonds into an irresistible snack. The most delicious almonds we have ever tasted, Marcona almonds, are imported from Spain.

● **MAKES 5 CUPS**

1 cup dried chickpeas

1½ cups dried fava beans

1 cup canola oil

1½ cups Marcona almonds or whole almonds

1 teaspoon sea salt

1 teaspoon sugar

¼ teaspoon ground cumin

¼ teaspoon cayenne

In separate bowls, soak the chickpeas and fava beans in a generous amount of cold water overnight.

Preheat the oven to 350°F.

Drain the chickpeas and fava beans. Rub the chickpeas between your hands just to loosen the skins. Pinch the fava beans on one end until the skin splits and squeeze out the bean.

Transfer the beans to a bowl and toss with the canola oil. Spread in a single layer on a 13 x 17-inch rimmed nonstick cookie sheet or regular cookie sheet greased with olive oil. If using Marcona almonds, bake the chickpeas and favas for 40 minutes, stirring once or twice, then add the almonds and bake for 5 minutes. If using whole almonds, bake the chickpeas and favas for 30 minutes, then add the almonds and bake for 15 minutes. The mixture should be golden brown and toasted.

Have ready a colander set over a bowl. Remove the mixture from the oven and transfer it to the colander to drain any oil. Transfer the mixture to paper towels and continue to drain for 3 minutes.

While still warm, toss the mixture with the salt, sugar, cumin, and cayenne. Cool to room temperature before serving. The nuts can be stored in an airtight container for up to 1 week.

WARM OCTOPUS WITH POTATOES AND SMOKED
PAPRIKA Smoked paprika, or *pimentón de la vera dulce,* is a classic ingredient from Spain. The peppers for the paprika are dried over slowly burning oak logs for days, sometimes weeks, before they are ground to a powder. The flavor goes very well with the subtle taste and meaty texture of octopus.

This recipe for cooking octopus is so easy. Most recipes ask that you dunk the octopus in boiling water a few times or tenderize it with a mallet. Cooking octopus in olive oil over low heat tenderizes it perfectly, giving it an unbelievable texture. • **SERVES 4 AS AN APPETIZER OR 2 AS A MAIN COURSE**

Cut the heads from the octopus and discard the heads. Cut the tentacles into individual pieces and put them in a medium saucepan. Cover the octopus with the 2 cups olive oil so that it is submerged. Set the pan over low heat and bring the temperature to 150°F as measured on an instant-read thermometer. Cook the octopus at this temperature until cooked through and tender when prodded with a fork, 40 to 45 minutes.

Meanwhile, put the potatoes in a small saucepan and add enough salted water to cover by 1 inch. Bring to a boil over medium heat and cook until the potato is tender when pierced with a knife, 10 to 15 minutes. Drain well.

Remove the octopus from the oil and transfer to paper towels to drain. Cut the tentacles into 1-inch pieces and transfer to a baking dish. Add the potatoes, garlic, paprika, and remaining 2 tablespoons olive oil. Season with salt and pepper and toss the ingredients to coat.

Preheat the broiler. Adjust the rack so that it is 6 inches from the heat.

Broil the octopus and potatoes for 4 minutes. Remove and serve immediately.

4 fresh or thawed baby octopus, 12 to 16 ounces each, rinsed

2 cups plus 2 tablespoons extra virgin olive oil

2 small Yukon Gold potatoes, peeled and cut into 1-inch dice

Sea salt and freshly ground black pepper

1 garlic clove, very thinly sliced

1/4 teaspoon smoked paprika

CHARRED BABY LEEKS WITH ROMESCO SAUCE The festival known as the Calçotada takes place in the Catalonia region of Spain in March, April, and May. Grown in special conditions through the winter months, the onions called *calçots* are charcoal grilled and served on terra-cotta roof tiles at countless restaurants and homes in the area. Diners' fingers turn black as they peel away the charred layers of the onion to get to the sweet inner bulb. Dipped into Romesco sauce, a puree of peppers, tomatoes, and nuts, and washed down with cava, they're addictive. Baby leeks are the closest thing we have found to a calçot in the United States, though long, thin spring onions or large scallions will also work. • **SERVES 4 AS AN APPETIZER OR SIDE DISH**

1 ancho chili

2 garlic cloves, peeled

1/3 cup whole almonds, preferably Marcona, toasted

1/3 cup blanched hazelnuts, toasted

Four 1/2-inch slices baguette, lightly toasted

2 roasted red bell peppers

4 plum tomatoes, peeled and seeded

1 tablespoon chopped flat-leaf parsley

Sea salt and freshly ground black pepper

1 tablespoon sherry vinegar

3/4 cup extra virgin olive oil

12 baby leeks or large scallions, trimmed

Put the ancho chili in a small bowl and cover with warm water. Let sit until softened, about 20 minutes. Drain, pat dry, halve, and seed the ancho.

To make the sauce, combine the ancho, garlic, almonds, hazelnuts, and bread in a food processor and puree until finely ground. Scrape down the sides of the bowl and add the roasted peppers, tomatoes, and parsley. Process until smooth and season with salt and pepper to taste. With the machine running, add the vinegar and then the olive oil in a slow stream. Process for at least 1 full minute to blend the ingredients and make a light and creamy sauce.

Pour the sauce into a medium bowl. It can be refrigerated overnight. Bring to room temperature before serving.

Prepare a fire in a charcoal grill.

Place the leeks directly on the coals for 3 to 4 minutes. Using tongs, flip them over and cook until they are blackened all over, 3 or 4 minutes.

To serve, place the leeks on a platter with the Romesco sauce alongside. Advise your guests to pull off the charred part of the leeks to reveal the soft inner bulb, which should be dipped into the sauce.

CATALONIAN PIZZA

Not that this pizza would ever exist in Catalonia, but it should. Here are all the classic flavors of the Costa Brava: chorizo, manchego cheese, tomatoes, and olive oil. • **MAKES FOUR 12-INCH PIZZAS**

Heat a medium sauté pan over medium heat. Add the chorizo and cook, breaking it up with a wooden spoon, until browned lightly and cooked through, 8 minutes. Remove from the heat and set aside to cool.

Have ready 2 nonstick cookie sheets or grease 2 regular cookie sheets with olive oil.

Preheat the oven to 500°F.

Divide the dough into 4 equal pieces. Working with one piece of dough at a time (cover the remaining dough with a moist kitchen towel until ready to use), flatten the dough on a floured work surface. Carefully stretch the dough out with your hands. Next, gently roll out the dough into a 12-inch circle about ⅛ inch thick.

Transfer the dough to a cookie sheet and brush with a thin layer of olive oil. Sprinkle 1 cup of the cheese over the dough, spreading it to the edge. Then make a layer of tomato slices and top with one-fourth of the chorizo. Season with salt and pepper. Repeat with a second ball of dough. Bake the pizzas until golden brown, 12 to 15 minutes. Remove from the oven and sprinkle some cilantro leaves on top. Repeat with the remaining 2 balls of dough to make 4 pizzas. Cut each pizza into 8 slices and serve.

1 pound bulk fresh chorizo sausage

Pizza Dough (page 86) or
2 pounds store-bought
refrigerated pizza dough

Extra virgin olive oil, for brushing

2 pounds manchego cheese,
shredded (4 cups)

4 large tomatoes, thinly sliced

Sea salt and freshly ground black
pepper

¼ cup fresh cilantro leaves

RAZOR CLAMS A LA PLANCHA

RAZOR CLAMS A LA PLANCHA Razor clams are uncommonly sweet and delicious and are becoming more available in American markets. The long, slender clams are aptly named for their resemblance to a straight-edge razor.

Bar La Punta in the seaside town of L'Escala on the Costa Brava in Spain is a casual, unassuming spot with its own fishing boat. Each day the owner sears the catch *a la plancha* on the flat iron cooktop of the range. The secret to his amazing seafood tapas, in addition to their impeccable freshness, is his use of olive oil, red wine vinegar, garlic, and parsley. This recipe also works well with shrimp, mussels, or scallops. • **SERVES 4 AS AN APPETIZER**

¼ cup plus 2 tablespoons extra virgin olive oil

2 tablespoons red wine vinegar

1 garlic clove, finely chopped

4 pounds razor clams

¼ cup finely chopped flat-leaf parsley

Combine the oil, vinegar, and garlic in a small bowl.

Heat a heavy sauté pan, preferably cast iron, over medium heat. After 5 minutes, place the clams in the pan and cook until the shells open and the clam meat becomes opaque, 2 to 3 minutes. Add about half of the garlic vinaigrette and cook for 1 minute.

Arrange the clams on a platter and spoon the pan juices on top. Add the parsley to the remaining vinaigrette and pour over the clams. Serve immediately.

FRIED EGGS WITH MUSHROOMS, GARLIC, AND PARSLEY

In the back of La Boqueria, the famous market on Las Ramblas in Barcelona, you will find the mushroom stall. The gentleman who runs this stall has the most incredible selection of mushrooms anywhere. The "counter" near his stall serves up the best mushrooms of the day sautéed with garlic and parsley with a couple of fresh market eggs cracked over the top. This is our rendition of breakfast in Barcelona at the market. • **SERVES 2 AS A MAIN COURSE**

Preheat the broiler to high.

Heat 2 tablespoons of the olive oil in a large ovenproof sauté pan over medium-high heat. Add the mushrooms and cover for 1 minute. Turn the mushrooms over, replace the cover, and cook until the mushrooms are browned evenly, 2 to 3 minutes more.

Meanwhile, combine the remaining tablespoon olive oil with the garlic and parsley.

With a spatula, move the mushrooms to the edges of the pan to make room for the eggs. Crack the eggs into the pan one at a time, being careful not to break the yolks. Cook until set on the bottom, about 2 minutes. Drizzle the garlic mixture over the eggs. Season with salt and pepper.

Place the pan under the broiler until the egg whites are set but the yolks are still runny, 2 to 3 minutes.

To serve, slide the eggs and mushrooms out of the pan onto plates.

3 tablespoons extra virgin olive oil

10 ounces mushrooms, preferably wild, such as chanterelles, morels, oyster, or shiitake, brushed clean and halved or quartered if large

2 garlic cloves, minced

1 tablespoon chopped flat-leaf parsley leaves

4 large eggs

Sea salt and freshly ground black pepper

WHITE ASPARAGUS SALAD Spaniards love white asparagus and don't have second thoughts about using asparagus coming from a jar. The best asparagus come from Navarra, a region in northern Spain also known for its rosé wines. Look for the Denominación Especifica mark on the label. These asparagus are prized for their smooth texture and balanced sweet, tangy taste.

This recipe transforms a reliable sherry vinaigrette, brightening it with tricolor peppers, shallot, egg, and capers. • **SERVES 4 AS A TASTING PORTION OR 2 AS AN APPETIZER OR SIDE DISH**

1 tablespoon plus 1 teaspoon sherry vinegar

Sea salt and freshly ground black pepper

¼ cup extra virgin olive oil

1 heaping tablespoon finely chopped red bell pepper

1 heaping tablespoon finely chopped yellow bell pepper

1 heaping tablespoon finely chopped green bell pepper

1 small shallot, finely chopped

1 hard-cooked egg, finely chopped

1½ tablespoons capers, preferably salted, rinsed and chopped

1 jar white asparagus, 8 to 10 very large spears, in water, preferably imported from Spain

Combine the vinegar and a pinch each of salt and pepper in a small bowl. In a slow stream, whisk the oil into the vinegar. Add the bell peppers, shallot, egg, and capers and combine. Allow the vegetables and dressing to marinate for 15 minutes.

Lay the asparagus on a serving dish. Spoon the marinated vegetables and vinaigrette over the asparagus and serve.

GARLIC SHRIMP WITH CHILIES AND ROSEMARY

GARLIC SHRIMP WITH CHILIES AND ROSEMARY It seems that you can find a version of this dish anywhere in the Mediterranean. Maybe that's because it's fast, simple, and delicious. Cutting the garlic into thin slices works well for this quick sauté. Any pickled or vinegar peppers will do, adding just the right amount of heat and acid. • **SERVES 4 AS AN APPETIZER OR 2 AS A MAIN COURSE**

3 tablespoons extra virgin olive oil

2 garlic cloves, thinly sliced

3 pounds shrimp (under 15 per pound), peeled and deveined

2 fresh rosemary sprigs

Sea salt and freshly ground black pepper

3 pickled chilies, such as spicy red peppers, halved

Heat the olive oil in a large sauté pan over medium-high heat. Add the garlic, let sizzle for 15 seconds, and then add the shrimp and rosemary. Season with salt and pepper. Cook for 2 to 3 minutes, turn the shrimp over, and cook until golden brown, about 1 minute.

Toss in the chilies. Transfer the shrimp to warm plates and top with the garlic, rosemary, chilies, and pan drippings. Serve immediately.

CARAJILLO After walking the market with our friend Isidre Girones as he buys items for his restaurant Ca L'Isidre, one of the best restaurants in Barcelona, we joined him for a morning carajillo. As we took our seat at the famous Bar Pinoxa counter, the friendly owner, with his megawatt smile and his tourist-pleasing "thumbs-up," prepared for us the best coffee drink ever. The carajillo is a mix of espresso, sugar, and rum—not just any rum, but Ron Pujol 1818 Gran Riserva, made right there in Catalonia. This is the perfect pick-me-up for a market morning, after lunch, after dinner . . . anytime. • **MAKES 1 DRINK**

1 teaspoon sugar

1/2 ounce dark rum

1 ounce brewed espresso

Put the sugar and rum in a cup. Pour in the espresso. Stir and enjoy.

CAVA AND THE WINES OF NORTHERN SPAIN

CAVA IS SPAIN'S SPARKLING WINE. Inspired by champagne and made in the same method, Metodo Tradicional cava ranges in flavors from dry to sweet.

By law, cava can be made from only up to five particular white grape varieties. Most cavas are made of a blend of these grapes and rarely from Chardonnay alone, even though it is one of the five grapes allowed. Almost all cava comes from Penedes, about thirty miles from Barcelona. As with champagne, cava that is nonvintage comes from a blend of different vintages, whereas a vintage-dated cava is made of wine from that particular vintage only. Cava uses the same terminology as champagne to describe the level of sweetness in the wine, such as *nature, brut, extra dry,* and so on. Most cava is made in the brut style.

Whereas we think of champagne or sparkling wine primarily as a celebratory drink, the Spaniards believe that cava is made to be enjoyed every day. In Spain, cava is sipped with tomato bread, garlic shrimp, and Serrano ham. Restaurants in Barcelona often serve a glass of the house cava after you place your order.

The best cavas have fresh, simple citrus flavors. When consumed young, cava is refreshing, earthy, and easy to drink. Less frothy than champagne or sparkling wines from California, cava also costs a fraction of the price. The best producers are Codorniu, Mont-Marcel, Segura Viudas, and Cristalino.

White Wines

One of the most fascinating and delicious still white wines comes from Galicia in northwestern Spain. Albariño, named for the grape, not for where it comes from (a rarity for wines in Spain), is relatively new in the international wine market. The first Albariño was exported to the United States in the late 1980s, and it was love at first sip.

Albariño has flavors of lemon, ginger, and almond. It can be creamy with a hint of honey or crisp and zingy with bright acidity and a touch of minerality. Albariño is complex, elegant, and seductive. It is unlike any other white wine. Best when drunk young, Albariño is great as a cocktail wine and fantastic with shellfish.

Albariño might be hard to find, but it's well worth the effort. Ask your wine shop to get the current vintage from any one of the following producers that we've seen here in the States: Martin Codax, Lusco, Lagar de Fornelos, Morgadio, Atio, and Burgans.

Two more white wines that also happen to be great values from Spain that we love are Alella Classico (made from Pansa Blanca and Xarel-lo grapes) from producer Parxet, and Rueda Superior (made from Verdejo blended with Sauvignon Blanc grapes) from producer Marqués de Riscal.

Red Wines

Rioja is Spain's greatest wine region and is the name of the well-known red wines made mostly from the Tempranillo grape. Blended with Garnacha, Graciano, and Mazuelo grapes, Rioja wines are earthy with plummy fruit and sweet spice aromas.

Rioja wines are categorized by quality and aging. Made with good-quality grapes and aged for at least two years, with one year in oak barrels, is Rioja Crianza. These wines are fruity and mouth filling, your everyday drinking red wine. Made from superior grapes from the best vineyards, Rioja Reserva must be aged for at least three years, one of which must be in oak barrels. Made only in the best years, these wines have luscious fruit, leather and tobacco in the nose, and an elegant long finish. Rioja Gran Reserva wines come from only the best grapes from the best vineyards, only in exceptional years. They must be aged for at least five years, two of which must be in oak barrels. These are the most powerful, refined, and complex Riojas, with aromas of vanilla and leather and flavors of concentrated black currants and spice.

Oak aging is crucial in giving Rioja its style and longevity. American and French oak barrels are preferred. And while traditionally longer aging than required has been the practice, modern winemakers in the Rioja are now focusing more on highlighting the fruit flavors.

A glass of Rioja pairs nicely with roast lamb, green or white asparagus, stuffed peppers, roasted potatoes, tomatoes, chorizo, roast duck, grilled quail, braised rabbit, thinly sliced Serrano ham, and all kinds of cheese. Look for wines from Bodegas Artadi, Bodegas Marqués de Murrieta, Muga, Martínez Bujanda, La Rioja Alta, Cune, Remelluri, Finca Allende, Bodegas Campo Viejo, Contino, and Telmo Rodriguez. All of these producers export to the United States.

Other reds from Spain to look for come from Ribera del Duero. Made with

Tinto Fino, a variation of Tempranillo, wines from this area explode with plum, black currant, leather, and vanilla flavors. Mouth filling and supple, these are unique and world-class wines.

Another group of red wines that is characteristic of a particular grape type and growing area is Priorat. Made mostly of Garnacha grapes, but blended with Carinena and sometimes Cabernet Sauvignon and Merlot, these reds are super-concentrated with ripe berry fruit, chocolate, and licorice flavors. Grown in wind-swept, rugged, and rocky terrain, the vines are painstakingly worked by hand, making the wines some of the most costly. When buying Priorat, keep in mind that these wines are considered the most intense and rarest wines produced in Spain.

Some of the best values in Spain can be found in Somontano and Navarra. Using native grapes as well as Cabernet Sauvignon, Merlot, Pinot Noir, and Syrah for the reds and Chardonnay and Gewürztraminer for the whites, Somontano and Navarra wines are worth seeking out for everyday consumption for their modern style and good prices. Navarra is also known for fresh, fruity rosés made from Garnacha grapes.

In our opinion, Spanish wines offer the greatest value in the market because of their amazing variety, high quality, and aging potential. They have an enormous affinity for food, all kinds of it, but can also be enjoyed as simply a beverage.

BLU DEL MONCENISIO

PARMIGIANO-REGGIANO

BOURGOGNE

BAMALOU

THE CHEESE PLATE

BONDE DE GÂTINE

CHAROLAIS

FIUM'ORBO DE BREBIS

GRANA PADANO

MANCHEGO

BRILLO DI TREVISO

BARILOTTO

VALENÇAY

GARROTXA

CACIOCAVALLO

SBRONZO

FIORE SARDO

EL SUSPIRO
DE CABRA

PONT L'EVEQUE

BRIN D'AMOUR

LA ROSSA
Soft Cheese
Product of Italy
CORA
Net Weight
3 oz. (100 g)

LA ROSSA

CIABOT

QUESO DE OVEJA PASTA
HNOS. PAJUELO BAUTISTA
ELABORADO EN ALMOHARIN

LA ROCHE

MUNSTER
GEROME

TORTA
DEL CASAR

CHEESE IS THE PERFECT wine bar food. You can have big hunks on hand and set out an assortment when needed. There are more high-quality domestic and imported cheeses available in American markets today than ever before. Here are some tips for creating a great cheese platter.

Choose cheeses made from different types of milk: cow, goat, and sheep.

Vary the ages and textures of the cheese. There should be soft, fresh, creamy young cheese; creamy yet firm slightly aged cheese, six months to one year; and hard cheese, aged one year or more. Varying the age will also help you select a range of flavors, from mild (fresh) to pungent (aged). Try to include a blue cheese in the mix, too.

Contrary to public opinion, red wine is not the only match for cheese. Whites go exceptionally well with goat cheese, and pungent blues go well with ports and other fortified wines.

When you purchase cheese, by all means taste it if at all possible. If not, give it a good whiff: if it smells like ammonia, it has not been stored properly and you

should pass it by. When you get the cheese home, keep it in its original wrapper in the refrigerator. Remember to take the cheese out of the refrigerator at least one hour before serving so it can warm up to room temperature. Cheese that is served too cold will not be as flavorful. If you do not finish all of the cheese, wrap it in fresh plastic wrap or aluminum foil and return it to the refrigerator.

In addition to bread, try serving your cheese with condiments such as nuts, salami, honey, fruit, and jellies. Honey, for example, works well with blue cheese. Nuts have an affinity for medium aged cheese. Fruit goes well with fresh cheese. Taste and experiment to find out what you like best.

Check out these cheeses!

BLU DEL MONCENISIO is a blue cow's milk cheese from Piedmont, Italy. The firmest of all the blues from Italy, it is rich, pungent, and delicious with honey.

PARMIGIANO-REGGIANO, the "King of Cheese," is a hard cow's milk cheese from Emilia-Romagna, Italy. Having an extraordinarily rich flavor and unique texture, it is delicious with Italian red wine, Franciacorta sparkling wine, or champagne.

CACIOCAVALLO is a cow's milk cheese from southern Italy. It is firm yet creamy with a sharp flavor.

GARROTXA is made of goat's milk in Catalonia, Spain. Creamy in texture, mild and nutty in flavor, this delightful cheese pairs well with Spanish white and red wines.

BOURGOGNE is a triple-cream cow's milk cheese from France. (*Triple-cream* means that cream is added to the full-fat milk when making the cheese.) Full flavored, smooth and rich, this cheese melts in your mouth. Good with full-bodied reds as well as sweet wines.

BAMALOU is a medium-firm cow's milk cheese from France.

BONDE DE GÂTINE is a goat's milk cheese from France. Dry and rustic, this cheese pairs beautifully with Sauvignon Blanc and other aromatic dry whites.

CHAROLAIS is a blend of cow's and goat's milk from Burgundy, France. It has a semisoft texture and a delightful sweet and salty flavor that sharpens with age. Pair it with Burgundian reds.

EL SUSPIRO DE CABRA is a creamy and luscious goat's milk cheese from Toledo, Spain.

FIORE SARDO is a hard sheep's milk cheese from Sardinia. Smoky in aroma and sharp in flavor, it goes well with Sardinian reds like Cannonau.

SBRONZO is buffalo milk cheese that is aged and rubbed with Aglianico grape skins and seeds from Italy. This is a sweet, creamy cheese with a red wine flavor. Try it with a glass of Aglianico wine from Campania.

FIUM'ORBO DE BREBIS is made from sheep's milk in France's Pyrenees Mountains. Its buttery and nutty flavors make it a fine match for full-bodied, fruity red wines.

GRANA PADANO is a cow's milk cheese from northern Italy. Named for its grainy texture, it is delicate and fragrant and can also be used for grating. It goes well with both white and red wines.

BRILLO DI TREVISO is a cow's milk cheese that has a wine-washed rind from Venice, Italy. It's a semisoft, tangy cheese with a creamy texture and fruity wine flavor that pairs well with most reds.

MANCHEGO is Spain's most famous sheep's milk cheese. Sold after three months of aging, the cheese is sweet and nutty. As it ages, it becomes more intense and pleasantly salty. It pairs well with Rioja and other Tempranillo-based wines.

CIABOT is a soft cheese made of a blend of sheep's and cow's milk in Piedmont, Italy. Named after the little stone houses farmers would use to ripen the cheese, it has aromas and flavors of milk and hay. Pair it with earthy Piedmontese red wines.

LA ROSSA is made from a blend of cow's and sheep's milk, the cheese wrapped in cherry leaves that have been steeped in brandy. Made in Italy, it is creamy and pungent with an intense, fruity aroma. Enjoy this cheese with a bit of the leaves. Decadent!

BRIN D'AMOUR is made with sheep's or goat's milk and is from the island of Corsica. The name means "a little bit of love." The cheese is rolled in dried rosemary and powdered juniper berries and chilies. The cheese has a soft texture and a delicate flavor that are delicious with the rosé wines of Côtes de Provence.

PONT L'EVEQUE is cow's milk cheese named after a town in Normandy, France, where it was first made in the thirteenth century. A semisoft cheese with an edible rind, it is savory and robust. It is great with French cider or Pinot Noir.

LA ROCHE is a creamy blue cow's milk cheese from France. It has a mild, balanced flavor with a sweet finish on the tongue. Try it with port, Muscat, or Banyuls wine.

BARILOTTO is made with buffalo milk and is classified as an aged ricotta from Salerno, Italy. It has a dry texture, similar to ricotta salata, and is subtle in flavor. Enjoy it with red wine.

MUNSTER GEROME is cow's milk cheese from Alsace, France. It is pungent, spicy, and earthy with a lemony tang. Enjoy it with the famed Alsatian wine Gewürztraminer.

VALENÇAY is goat's milk cheese from the Loire, France. A classic goat cheese in pyramid form covered in ash, it has a dense, smooth texture and a delightful crisp tang. Enjoy this cheese with a crisp Sauvignon Blanc or Chardonnay.

TORTA DEL CASAR is a sheep's milk cheese from the western central part of Spain. A very rich and creamy cheese with a strong and pungent taste, it is best spread on bread due to its delightfully gooey texture. To serve, slice off the top and spoon out the cheese. Serve with Pedro Ximénez sherry.

NICE

PARTY ON THE RIVIERA

T

HIS CHAPTER is all about the Mediterranean diet with a French accent. Although these flavor-packed recipes promote good health, you will never feel denied. Pair them with the enjoyable dry rosé wines of the region; we highlight the virtues of these often misunderstood wines that are ideal with these recipes.

Riviera Wine Cooler

Raw Winter Vegetable Salad with Anchovy Sauce

Goat Cheese and Fava Bean Crostini

Tuna Tartare with Rice Beans

Crispy Potato Cake with Lemon and Parsley

Pea, Bacon, and Pecorino Salad

Grilled Summer Vegetables with Pistou

Flatbread with Chickpea Puree, Fried Garlic, and Fried Parsley

Braised Chicken with Niçoise Olives and Orange

Lavender Ice Cream Sandwiches on Brioche

Chocolate and Banyuls Truffles

Dry Rosés—Some of the Best Food Wines

RIVIERA WINE COOLER While having lunch in Nice, France, one incredibly hot summer day, thirsty but thinking that the wine of the region was probably not going to quench our thirst, we asked our waiter if he could recommend something that might do the trick. *"Mais bien sûr,"* he replied. The following recipe is what he then served us.

- **MAKES 1 COCKTAIL**

Shake the wine, simple syrup, and lime juice with ice in a cocktail shaker. Strain over ice into a large wineglass.

4 ounces dry white wine, preferably Sauvignon Blanc or Sémillon

1 1/2 ounces Simple Syrup (recipe follows)

1 1/2 ounces fresh lime juice

SIMPLE SYRUP
MAKES ABOUT 1 CUP

Combine the sugar with 3/4 cup cold water in a small saucepan. Bring to a boil over high heat and stir to dissolve the sugar. Once the sugar has dissolved, remove the pan from the heat and let cool completely. The syrup can be stored in a covered container in the refrigerator for several weeks.

3/4 cup sugar

HONEY SIMPLE SYRUP
Substitute honey for the sugar.

RAW WINTER VEGETABLE SALAD WITH ANCHOVY SAUCE

This is a great way to enjoy your vegetables during the winter. Choose winter white vegetables and slice them thinly on a mandoline or by hand. A hearty anchovy and garlic sauce is mellowed a bit by milk. • **SERVES 6 AS A TASTING PORTION OR 4 AS AN APPETIZER**

³/₄ cup anchovy fillets packed in salt, rinsed

5 garlic cloves, peeled

1 cup plus 3 tablespoons whole milk

4 medium fresh mushrooms, brushed clean

¹/₂ fennel bulb, trimmed

1 head of Belgian endive

2 fresh hearts of palm

One 2-ounce block of Parmigiano-Reggiano cheese

2 tablespoons extra virgin olive oil

Juice of ¹/₂ lemon

Sea salt and freshly ground white pepper

Combine the anchovies, garlic, and 1 cup of the milk in a small saucepan over low heat and cook for 1 hour. Strain, reserving the liquid.

In a food processor or blender, puree the anchovies and garlic with 1 tablespoon of the reserved liquid plus the remaining 3 tablespoons milk until smooth. The dressing should be somewhat thick but pourable. It can be refrigerated overnight. Bring to room temperature before serving.

Thinly slice the mushrooms, fennel, endive, hearts of palm, and cheese and combine in a medium bowl. Toss with the olive oil and lemon juice. Divide equally among 4 to 6 plates. Make a ring around each salad on the plate with the anchovy sauce. Season the salad with a pinch of salt and a grind of pepper. Serve immediately.

GOAT CHEESE AND FAVA BEAN CROSTINI This recipe is all about quality ingredients. Look for the freshest, creamiest goat cheese and the youngest, smallest fava beans for this dish. Drizzled with fine extra virgin olive oil and a couple of twists of black pepper, these crostini are simple and satisfying. We first enjoyed this dish in Monte Carlo. We think you will be as amazed as we were at how good just a few great ingredients can taste. • **MAKES 12 CROSTINI**

Shuck the long fava bean pods to free the individual beans. Soak the beans in cold water for 30 minutes, then drain and peel.

Preheat the broiler.

Place the bread slices on a cookie sheet and toast under the broiler, watching closely so they do not burn, about 1 minute. Turn the bread over and repeat. Remove from the oven.

While the toasts are still warm, but cool enough to handle, spread each piece with a generous amount of goat cheese. Toss the fava beans with the olive oil and season to taste with salt and pepper. Evenly distribute the fava beans over the crostini, drizzling any remaining oil over the top. Serve immediately, offering freshly ground pepper at the table.

$1^1/_2$ **pounds fresh fava beans**

Twelve $^1/_2$-inch-thick baguette slices

8 ounces goat cheese

$^1/_4$ **cup extra virgin olive oil**

Sea salt and freshly ground black pepper

TUNA TARTARE WITH RICE BEANS

Tuna tartare—diced raw tuna—is all about showcasing great, sushi-quality fish. When we created this dish, we thought about adding rice as a component, as a nod to sushi. But, in keeping with the Mediterranean soul of this book, we hit upon the idea of rice beans, little-known delicious small (hence the name) beans from the French Riviera. If you can't find these beans, substitute the smallest white beans you can find. We take the Mediterranean flavors further by adding olives, capers, basil, tomatoes, and olive oil. • **SERVES 4 AS AN APPETIZER OR 2 AS A MAIN COURSE**

$^3/_4$ cup dried rice beans

$^1/_4$ cup plus 2 tablespoons extra virgin olive oil

1 pound sushi-grade tuna, cut into $^1/_2$-inch dice

1 plum tomato, peeled, seeded, and diced

1 small shallot, minced

$^1/_4$ cup chopped pitted alfonso or kalamata olives

2 tablespoons capers, preferably salted, rinsed and patted dry

4 large fresh basil leaves, torn into small pieces

Grated zest of $^1/_2$ lemon

3 tablespoons fresh lemon juice

Sea salt and freshly ground black pepper

Put the rice beans in a medium saucepan over medium-high heat and add enough water to cover by 2 inches. Boil until tender, about 45 minutes. Drain the beans and let cool completely. Stir in 1 tablespoon of the olive oil and refrigerate until ready to use, up to overnight.

In a large bowl, combine the tuna, tomato, shallot, olives, capers, basil, lemon zest, lemon juice, and remaining 5 tablespoons olive oil. Season to taste with salt and pepper.

To serve, spoon the rice beans into shallow bowls and top with the tuna mixture.

CRISPY POTATO CAKE WITH LEMON AND PARSLEY The

French have a way with potatoes. Consider the fry, or *frite,* which has achieved world-wide celebrity status. Or mashed potatoes, gratins of all kinds, roasted new potatoes...

This potato cake is another great French recipe that was inspired by dinner years ago at the venerable Parisian restaurant L'Ami Louis. Crisp and light, these potato cakes need to be cooked in a small cast-iron pan if you want to duplicate the effect created in the 150-year-old wood-fired ovens of the restaurant. Be sure to drizzle the garlic, parsley, and lemon oil over the cake right out of the oven for an incredibly aromatic presentation.

- **SERVES 4 AS A TASTING PORTION OR 2 AS A SIDE DISH**

Put the potatoes in a medium saucepan and add enough water to cover by 1 inch. Bring to a boil over medium-high heat and cook until just tender, 6 to 7 minutes. Drain well and let cool slightly. Season with salt and pepper.

Preheat the oven to 400°F.

Heat a 6½-inch ovenproof sauté pan, preferably cast iron, over medium heat for 3 to 4 minutes. Add 2 tablespoons of the olive oil and heat until the oil begins to smoke lightly, about 2 minutes. Carefully press all of the potatoes firmly into the pan and drizzle 1 tablespoon of the remaining oil over the top. Reduce the heat to medium-low and cook until the bottom is lightly browned, 15 to 20 minutes.

Transfer the pan to the oven and bake for 15 minutes. Remove the pan from the oven, cover with a plate, and flip the potato cake onto the plate. Slide the potato cake, brown side up, back into the pan, smashing the cake with a spatula if necessary to fit. Cook over medium heat on the stovetop to brown the other side, 10 to 15 minutes.

Combine the parsley, lemon zest, garlic, and remaining tablespoon of oil in a small bowl. Flip the potato cake onto a plate and drizzle with the parsley mixture. Cut into wedges and serve immediately.

3 medium Yukon Gold potatoes, peeled and cut into 2-inch chunks

Sea salt and freshly ground black pepper

¼ cup extra virgin olive oil

1 teaspoon chopped flat-leaf parsley

¼ teaspoon grated lemon zest

⅛ teaspoon minced garlic

PEA, BACON, AND PECORINO SALAD
Three parts of the pea plant are featured in this hearty spring salad: the pea itself (both shelled peas and sugar snaps); the shoot, which is the tender green leaf or tendrils of the pea plant; and the pea sprout, which is the beginning stage of the plant. If you cannot find pea shoots or tendrils at your local farmers' market, substitute any tender spring greens in their place. Enjoy this salad with a dry, crisp white wine such as a Sauvignon Blanc. • **SERVES 6 AS AN APPETIZER OR 4 AS A SIDE DISH**

6 strips bacon, cut crosswise into $^1/_2$-inch slices

$^1/_3$ cup plus 2 tablespoons extra virgin olive oil

2 slices bread, crust removed, cut into $^1/_4$-inch dice

Sea salt

1 cup fresh peas

1 cup sugar snap peas, thinly sliced

$^1/_2$ cup pea shoots, cut in half

$^1/_2$ cup pea sprouts

1 tablespoon fresh lemon juice

12 thin slices Pecorino Romano cheese, optional

Preheat the oven to 350°F.

Cook the bacon in a sauté pan over medium heat until crisp but still chewy, 5 to 6 minutes. Drain the bacon on paper towels. Reserve 3 teaspoons of the bacon fat in a large bowl.

Wipe out the sauté pan and return to medium-high heat. Add $^1/_3$ cup of the oil. Add a cube of bread to test the temperature. When the cube starts to sizzle and fry, add the remaining cubes and fry until light golden brown, tossing occasionally, 4 to 5 minutes. Transfer the croutons to paper towels to drain.

Have ready a bowl of ice water. Bring a saucepan of lightly salted water to a boil over medium-high heat. Add the fresh peas and boil for 30 seconds. Scoop out the peas with a slotted spoon and plunge them into the ice water. Repeat with the snap peas. When cooled completely, drain the peas and snap peas well.

Add the peas, snap peas, pea shoots, pea sprouts, and croutons to the bowl with the bacon fat. Add the lemon juice and remaining 2 tablespoons olive oil and toss well. Divide the salad among 4 to 6 plates. Top each salad with 2 or 3 thin shavings of cheese, if using, and some crumbled bacon. Serve immediately.

GRILLED SUMMER VEGETABLES WITH PISTOU This dish can be served warm or at room temperature, making it the perfect summertime starter or side dish for a relaxed lunch or dinner. We recommend grilling the vegetables on their own—naked, if you will—and then adding the dressing after you have grilled the vegetables so they soak up all of its fresh flavor.

Pistou is the French version of pesto, the main difference being the addition of tomato and Gouda cheese to the bright green sauce. • **SERVES 6 AS AN APPETIZER OR SIDE DISH**

4 1/2 cups fresh basil leaves

2 garlic cloves, smashed and peeled

1/4 cup extra virgin olive oil

2 plum tomatoes, coarsely chopped

Sea salt and freshly ground black pepper

3/4 cup grated aged Gouda cheese

2 large zucchini, sliced lengthwise

1 large eggplant, sliced into circles

1 medium red bell pepper, quartered

1 medium yellow bell pepper, quartered

1 large sweet onion, sliced into 1/4-inch rings

4 medium portobello mushroom caps, brushed clean

6 scallions

To make the pistou, puree the basil, garlic, and olive oil in a food processor or blender until smooth, about 1 minute. Transfer to a small bowl and stir in the tomatoes. Season with salt and pepper to taste. Mix in the cheese. The pistou can be refrigerated overnight. Bring to room temperature before serving.

Prepare a fire in a charcoal grill or preheat a gas grill to medium-high heat.

Working in batches, grill the zucchini, eggplant, bell peppers, onion, mushrooms, and scallions until well marked, 3 to 4 minutes on each side.

Arrange the vegetables on a platter and season with salt and pepper. Spoon the pistou over the vegetables. Serve hot, warm, or at room temperature.

FLATBREAD WITH CHICKPEA PUREE, FRIED GARLIC, AND FRIED PARSLEY

This could be called Hummus Pizza. Dusting the flatbread with sumac before serving adds a beautiful color and pleasing citrus tang. See photograph on page 144; see the Resource Guide, page 194, for where to buy sumac. • **MAKES 16 LARGE PIECES**

Puree the chickpeas with 1/3 cup of the oil in a food processor until smooth. Season to taste with salt and pepper.

Heat the remaining 3 tablespoons oil in a medium sauté pan over medium-high heat. Add the garlic and cook until golden brown, 2 to 3 minutes. Add parsley leaves and fry until crisp, 2 to 3 minutes. Remove the pan from the heat and set aside to cool.

Preheat the oven to 425°F.

Transfer the rolled-out dough to 2 nonstick cookie sheets, or grease regular cookie sheets with olive oil, so that 2 pieces will fit on each cookie sheet. The pieces should be approximately 4 inches wide and 12 inches long. Brush lightly with the garlic-parsley oil and bake until golden brown, 10 to 12 minutes. Remove from the oven.

Spread the flatbreads with a generous layer of chickpea puree and sprinkle with garlic chips and fried parsley. Return to the oven until warmed through, 2 to 3 minutes. Remove from the oven. Dust with sumac and serve.

Two 15-ounce cans chickpeas, rinsed and drained

1/3 cup plus 3 tablespoons extra virgin olive oil

Sea salt and freshly ground black pepper

4 garlic cloves, thinly sliced

1/2 cup flat-leaf parsley leaves

Crispy Parmigiano Flatbread dough (page 20), rolled but not sprinkled with cheese

1/4 teaspoon powdered sumac

BRAISED CHICKEN WITH NIÇOISE OLIVES AND ORANGE

The flavors in this recipe are a classic French combination, but a touch of orange wakes everything up. Small and purplish in color, Niçoise olives have a nutty, mellow flavor and are most associated with the cuisine of the Provence region in France. For equally terrific results, this dish can be prepared with rabbit in place of the chicken. • **SERVES 4 AS A MAIN COURSE**

3 tablespoons extra virgin olive oil

One 3½-pound chicken, cut into 8 pieces

1 medium carrot, chopped

1 celery stalk, chopped

½ medium onion, chopped

1 garlic clove, sliced

1 cup dry red wine

1 large orange

2½ cups low-sodium chicken broth

1 bay leaf

2 fresh thyme sprigs

½ cup Niçoise olives

Heat the olive oil in a large sauté pan or Dutch oven over medium-high heat. Working in batches, add the chicken and brown on all sides, about 10 minutes per batch. Transfer to a plate and set aside.

Add the carrot, celery, onion, and garlic to the pan. Cook until slightly browned, about 2 minutes. Add the wine and stir to loosen the browned bits from the bottom of the pan.

Remove the zest from the orange in wide strips using a vegetable peeler or knife. Add the chicken broth, bay leaf, thyme, and orange zest to the pan. Return the chicken pieces to the pan, cover, and simmer over low heat until cooked through and tender, about 1 hour.

Meanwhile, section the orange. Cut the top and bottom off the orange, exposing the flesh. Stand the orange on one end and, following the curve of the fruit, slice away the pith and a little of the flesh. Pick up the orange in one hand and with a paring knife in the other, working over a bowl, slice between the membranes to release the orange segments. Squeeze the membrane to release any juice and then discard the membrane.

Transfer the chicken to a large platter and keep warm. Strain the sauce into a clean saucepan over medium-high heat and boil to reduce the sauce by half, about 5 minutes. Discard the vegetables. Remove the sauce from the heat and add the orange segments, orange juice, and olives. Top the chicken with the olives, oranges, and sauce and serve immediately.

LAVENDER ICE CREAM SANDWICHES ON BRIOCHE The
beautiful purple flower that is one of the ingredients in the popular herbes de Provence seasoning blend, lavender infuses ice cream for these irresistible dessert sandwiches.

• **SERVES 8**

Bring the cream, milk, and lavender flowers to a simmer in a large heavy-bottomed saucepan over medium heat. Remove the pan from the heat, cover, and let steep for 30 minutes.

Pour the cream mixture through a fine-mesh sieve into a clean saucepan. Discard the lavender.

Fill a large bowl halfway with ice water and nestle a medium bowl in the ice bath.

Meanwhile, whisk the egg yolks and sugar in a large bowl until pale in color. While whisking, slowly add 1 cup of the hot cream. When blended, return the entire mixture to the saucepan and cook over medium-low heat, stirring constantly, until the custard thickens and coats the back of a spoon, up to 15 minutes.

Strain the custard into the medium bowl, return it to the ice bath, and let cool completely, stirring occasionally. Remove from the ice bath, cover, and refrigerate until cold, at least 2 hours or overnight.

Transfer the custard to an ice cream maker and process according to the manufacturer's instructions. Transfer the ice cream to a covered container and put in the freezer until firm.

Split the rolls or cut the loaf into sixteen $1/2$-inch-thick slices. Scoop the ice cream into the brioche rolls or between 2 slices of bread and dust with confectioners' sugar. Sprinkle with edible lavender flowers. Serve immediately.

3 cups heavy cream

$1^1/2$ cups whole milk

3 tablespoons dried edible lavender flowers, plus more for serving

8 large egg yolks

$3/4$ cup sugar

8 small fresh brioche rolls, or one 9 x 5-inch loaf

Confectioners' sugar, for garnish

CHOCOLATE AND BANYULS TRUFFLES Banyuls adds sweetness and fruit flavors to these rich, delicious, melt-in-your-mouth chocolate truffles. Banyuls is a fortified wine made from Grenache Noir grapes (the best are made with 100 percent) grown in southwestern France on terraced hills above the Mediterranean Sea. Reddish in color and redolent of dried plums and caramel, Banyuls has flavors of ripe red fruit, coffee, and chocolate. It is lighter in body than port but rich and intense. Traditionally it is served with all kinds of chocolate as well as chocolate desserts. Look for producers Les Clos de Paulilles, M. Chapoutier, Domaine du Mas Blanc, La Tour Vieille, and Cornet et Cie. • **MAKES ABOUT 3 DOZEN TRUFFLES**

10 ounces bittersweet chocolate, finely chopped

1 cup heavy cream

3½ tablespoons unsalted butter, softened

¼ cup Banyuls wine

½ cup unsweetened cocoa powder, preferably Dutch processed, or more if needed

Put the chocolate in a large heatproof bowl.

Bring the cream to a boil in a small saucepan over medium heat. Pour the cream into the bowl of chocolate. Using a whisk in concentric circles, stir the cream into the chocolate until the chocolate is melted and the mixture is smooth, 2 minutes. Add half the butter at a time, stirring gently to combine. Stir in the Banyuls.

Transfer the mixture to a bowl and refrigerate until well chilled, at least 2 hours or overnight.

Sprinkle the cocoa powder into a medium bowl.

Remove the truffle mixture from the refrigerator. Using a melon baller or a teaspoon, scoop up the chocolate and transfer to a cookie sheet lined with parchment. Dust your palms with some cocoa powder and, one by one, shape the chocolate into balls. Drop the balls into the cocoa powder a few at a time and toss to coat. Remove the truffles from the cocoa powder, shake off the excess cocoa, and return to the parchment-lined cookie sheet. Repeat the process, adding more cocoa powder to the bowl if needed, until all the truffles have been coated with cocoa powder.

The truffles can be served immediately or refrigerated in an airtight container for up to 2 days. Serve the truffles chilled or at cool room temperature.

DRY ROSÉS ARE SOME OF THE BEST WINES to enjoy with food. Rosés complement chicken, pork, cured meats, seafood, dips and spreads, garlic, spices, salads, and vegetables. They pair nicely with full-flavored and spicy dishes and are satisfying on those warm summer days when a glass of white or red just won't do. Aromatic, thirst quenching and pretty, rosé wines can range in color from light pink to copper hued to light red.

In the Mediterranean, it is common to drink rosés, especially when it's hot. Not only is a glass of chilled rosé refreshing (and rosé should always be served chilled) but because of the contact with the grape skins that give them color, the wine also picks up some of the alluring flavors of red wine.

In France, Provence is the region most famous for its dry rosés. Made from Mourvèdre, Cinsaut, Grenache, Syrah, and other red grapes, these wines explode with strawberry fruit and lively acidity but finish bone dry on the tongue. Wines with this kind of acidity and dryness make you want to take a bite of food and then call you back for another sip of wine. In the southern Rhône region, the rosé known as Tavel is also highly prized.

Spain takes its rosé wines seriously. Known as *rosados,* many are made with Garnacha, but they can also be made with Tempranillo and Cabernet Sauvignon. Faint in color, but juicy in flavor, rosado from Navarra in northern Spain is one of the country's best.

Rosés are available in wine shops mostly during the warm months. Many producers here in the United States are now crafting rosé wines with less sweetness. In California, traditional Rhône varietal producers are making rosés in the European style. You can also find American rosés made from Syrah, Sangiovese, Pinot Noir, the Cabernets, and Merlot. Look for dry rosé from California producers Bonny Doon, Eberle, Iron Horse, Saintsbury, Swanson, and Preston, to name just a few.

LISBON

OLD-WORLD CHARM

E VEN THOUGH PORTUGAL is not a Mediterranean country, it feels like one. These typical Portuguese-seasoned recipes bring something old and new to the meal. Discover a delicious menu of bold yet familiar flavors, paired with Portuguese wines.

Mini Sobresada Puffs

Bacalhau Fritters with Aïoli

Grilled Squid Piri-Piri

Smoked Mackerel Spread

Iberian Vegetable Salad

Caldo Verde

Angel Hair with Clams, Chorizo, Saffron, Orange, Tomato, and Cilantro

Portuguese Seafood Stew

The Surprising Wines of Portugal

MINI SOBRESADA PUFFS Traveling up into the hills surrounding Lisbon, we kept wondering if we did indeed have the right address as the taxi climbed higher and higher. Our destination was a restaurant that came highly recommended by our friend Les Pinsof, who possesses one of the best palates of anyone we know and can find great, unpretentious local food anywhere.

When we finally arrived at Mercado de Peixe, our waiter guided us by the open kitchen and past the fresh fish displayed on top of crushed ice in marble bins. Waiting for us at our tables were these incredible sobresada-filled rolls, creamy rounds of cheese, and platters of local jamón, all this just to make sure that we could endure the wait until the cooks finished grilling our fish selection. Though we're sure it was fabulous, we can't really remember the fish that we had traveled so far to eat. What we do remember are these rolls. • **MAKES 16 PUFFS**

Have ready 2 nonstick muffin tins or grease regular muffin tins with olive oil.

Transfer the pizza dough sheets to a cutting board and cut the dough into sixteen 2-inch squares. Sprinkle some sausage and cheese in the center of each square. Pull the edges of each square together toward the middle, pinching to seal. Form into a ball by rolling gently in your hands and place each puff, seam side down, into 1 cup in the muffin pan. Let rise in a warm place for 30 minutes.

Preheat the oven to 400°F.

Brush each puff lightly with olive oil. Bake until golden brown, about 15 minutes. Serve warm or at room temperature.

Wrapped in an airtight container, these puffs can be refrigerated for 2 to 3 days or frozen for up to 1 week. To reheat, wrap the puffs in foil and heat at 350°F for 8 minutes.

1/2 recipe Pizza Dough (page 86) or 1 pound store-bought refrigerated pizza dough, rolled out

1/3 cup diced Portuguese sobresada, Italian soppressata, or other dried sausage

1/3 cup diced Asiago cheese

Extra virgin olive oil, for brushing

BACALHAU FRITTERS WITH AÏOLI This may be our favorite way to eat salt cod. Mixed with creamy potatoes, breaded, and fried, these warm, crispy-on-the-outside, soft-on-the-inside fritters are positively addictive.

The Portuguese love these fritters so much that rumor has it the Portuguese national soccer team traveled to Germany for the 2006 World Cup with their own personal chef in tow to prepare them. See photograph on page 161. • **MAKES 28 FRITTERS**

1 pound salt cod

2 large baking potatoes, peeled and cut into 1-inch pieces

1 small onion, chopped

2 cups whole milk, or more to cover

Sea salt and freshly ground white pepper

4 large eggs

1 cup all-purpose flour

2 cups dried bread crumbs, preferably panko

1 quart canola oil

Aïoli (recipe follows)

Soak the cod in cold water in the refrigerator for 2 to 3 days, changing the water twice a day to remove excess salt.

Drain the cod, cut it into 1-inch pieces, and put it in a large saucepan with the potatoes and onion. Add the milk to cover and simmer over medium heat until the cod is falling apart, the potatoes are cooked through, and the onion is soft, about 20 minutes. Drain and cool the mixture.

Pass the potatoes through a ricer and set aside. Process the cod and the onions in a food processor until shredded. In a large bowl, combine the cod and potatoes. Season to taste with salt (if necessary) and white pepper.

Beat the eggs in a shallow bowl. Put the flour in a second bowl and the bread crumbs in a third.

Scoop heaping tablespoons of the cod mixture and form into small balls with your hands. Dip the balls in the eggs, then in the flour, and then in the bread crumbs, shaking off any excess. At this point the balls can be refrigerated overnight.

To fry, heat the canola oil in a deep-fryer or heavy-bottomed pot to 325°F.

Working in batches, carefully deep-fry the balls in the hot oil, turning to cook evenly, until golden brown, 4 to 5 minutes.

Remove the fritters from the oil and drain on paper towels. When cool enough to handle, about 3 minutes, transfer to a serving plate. Serve with the aïoli on the side for dipping.

AÏOLI

MAKES ABOUT 1½ CUPS

Puree the egg yolks, lemon juice, and garlic with 1 table-spoon water in a blender or food processor. With the machine running, drizzle in the olive oil and process until well combined. Add the salt. Refrigerate until ready to use or for up to 1 day.

2 large egg yolks

2 tablespoons fresh lemon juice

2 garlic cloves, minced

1 cup extra virgin olive oil

½ teaspoon sea salt

GRILLED SQUID PIRI-PIRI Piri-piri sauce is like ketchup to the Portuguese. They sprinkle it on everything from french fries to eggs. The marinade and sauce for the squid in this recipe uses piri-piri sauce from a bottle as a base but adds other ingredients like brandy to re-create a full-flavored marinade that can also be used for chicken or fish. Look for bottled piri-piri in gourmet markets or see the Resource Guide (page 194). If using wood skewers, be sure to soak them in water before threading the squid onto them to prevent burning. • **SERVES 4 AS AN APPETIZER**

Rinse the squid and pat dry.

With scissors, make 4 cuts across the body of each piece of squid as if you were going to cut them into rings, but leave them attached on one side. You should have 5 rings held together on one side. Cut open the second and fourth rings of each piece. The body should still be intact.

In a shallow nonreactive bowl, combine 1 teaspoon of the piri-piri sauce with 1 tablespoon of the brandy and the garlic. Add the squid bodies and tentacles, cover, and refrigerate for 4 to 8 hours.

Prepare a charcoal grill or preheat a gas grill to medium-high heat.

Remove the squid from the marinade, shaking off any excess. Thread the squid bodies and tentacles onto 4 skewers. Grill until browned and well marked, about 3 minutes on each side. Be careful not to overcook the squid or it will become tough.

To make the sauce, combine the remaining 2 teaspoons piri-piri, remaining 2 tablespoons brandy, and the oil in a small bowl and whisk until well blended.

Place the grilled squid on a warm platter and drizzle with the sauce. Serve immediately.

1 pound large squid (5 to 8 inches long each), bodies and tentacles separated

1 tablespoon piri-piri sauce

3 tablespoons brandy

1 garlic clove, thinly sliced

1/4 cup extra virgin olive oil

SMOKED MACKEREL SPREAD Wildly popular in Spain and Portugal, rich Spanish mackerel is full of omega-3 fatty acids, the good fats. This recipe for a creamy spread mellows the pronounced flavor of the mackerel while still celebrating all that makes it delicious.

If using peppered mackerel, scrape off the seasonings before using the fish. Serve this spread with plenty of thin slices of toasted baguette or crackers. • **MAKES ABOUT 2 CUPS**

7 ounces smoked mackerel fillets, skinned

1/2 cup heavy cream

1/4 cup cream cheese

3 tablespoons cornichons, chopped

1/2 small shallot, minced

3 hard-cooked eggs, coarsely chopped

Puree the mackerel, cream, and cream cheese in a food processor until smooth and light, 45 seconds to 1 minute. Transfer to a bowl and stir in the cornichons and shallot. Gently stir in the eggs just to combine.

Scrape into a small serving dish or bowl and refrigerate for at least 1 hour and up to 1 day. Let sit at room temperature for 15 to 30 minutes before serving to soften.

IBERIAN VEGETABLE SALAD This simple Mediterranean salad is perfect for lunch or as a light dinner with a glass of crisp Alvarinho. • **SERVES 4 AS AN APPETIZER**

2 medium Idaho potatoes, peeled and quartered

4 green bell peppers

2 medium ripe tomatoes, quartered

1 small sweet onion, thinly sliced and separated into rings

Sherry Vinaigrette (page 102)

Salt and freshly ground black pepper

Put the potatoes in a medium saucepan and add enough water to cover by 1 inch. Bring the potatoes to a boil over medium-high heat and cook until tender, about 20 minutes. Drain and let cool.

Meanwhile, roast the peppers over an open flame (or underneath the broiler), turning with tongs as needed, until blackened all over, 12 minutes. Transfer to a paper bag or bowl and close the bag or cover the bowl with plastic wrap. Let sit for 15 minutes. Core, peel, quarter, and seed the peppers.

Arrange the potatoes, tomatoes, and peppers on a large platter, alternating colors. Top with the onion rings. Drizzle with some of the vinaigrette. Pass the salt, pepper, and extra vinaigrette at the table.

CALDO VERDE The national dish of Portugal, *caldo verde,* a soulful soup, is found in all types of restaurants throughout the country. Like many great soups and stews, this soup actually tastes better the day after it is made. • **SERVES 6 AS AN APPETIZER OR 4 AS A MAIN COURSE**

Heat the olive oil in a large pot over medium-high heat. Add the chorizo and cook until browned, about 3 minutes. Remove from the pot and set aside on a plate. Add the onion and garlic to the pot and cook until soft, 3 to 5 minutes. Add the kale, cover the pot, and cook until the greens wilt, 3 to 5 minutes. Add the broth. Reduce the heat to medium-low and simmer, covered, for 1 hour.

Add the potatoes and simmer until nearly tender, about 10 minutes. Add the sausage and simmer for 5 minutes. Season with salt and pepper to taste and serve immediately or refrigerate for up to a few days and reheat thoroughly before serving.

2 tablespoons extra virgin olive oil

12 ounces fresh chorizo sausage, about 3 links, cut into $1/4$-inch coins

1 large onion, chopped

5 garlic cloves, smashed and peeled

1 pound kale, stems removed, leaves cut crosswise into $1/2$-inch strips

6 cups low-sodium chicken broth

2 medium Yukon Gold potatoes, peeled and cut into $1/2$-inch pieces

Sea salt and freshly ground black pepper

ANGEL HAIR WITH CLAMS, CHORIZO, SAFFRON, ORANGE, TOMATO, AND CILANTRO
This dish is a classic Portuguese combination of clams and pork with the added Mediterranean ingredients of saffron, orange, and tomato finished, only as an Italian would, with angel hair pasta to soak up all the amazing flavors. • **SERVES 6 AS AN APPETIZER OR 4 AS A MAIN COURSE**

3 tablespoons extra virgin olive oil

8 ounces fresh bulk chorizo sausage or, if in links, casing removed

2 large garlic cloves, thinly sliced

1 pound clams, preferably Manila, well scrubbed

1 cup low-sodium chicken broth

3/4 cup fresh orange juice

1 medium bay leaf

Pinch of saffron threads

Sea salt and freshly ground black pepper

1 pound angel hair pasta

3 oranges, cut into segments (see page 62)

1 large beefsteak tomato or 4 plum tomatoes, peeled, seeded, and chopped

2 tablespoons whole cilantro leaves

Bring a large pot of lightly salted water to a boil.

Heat the olive oil in a large sauté pan over medium-high heat. Add the chorizo and cook, breaking it up with a wooden spoon, until browned, 5 to 6 minutes. Add the garlic and cook for 1 minute. Add the clams, chicken broth, orange juice, bay leaf, and saffron. Cover and cook until all the clams open, 7 to 8 minutes. Season to taste with salt and pepper.

Add the pasta to the boiling water and cook until al dente, about 2 minutes less than what the box advises. Drain the pasta and return to the pot. Pour the clam mixture into the pot, place over low heat, and toss the pasta with the sauce for 1 minute to allow it to marry with the sauce and absorb some of it. Add the orange segments and chopped tomato, toss, and cook for another minute. The pasta should still be firm to the bite.

Transfer the pasta to a warm platter. Remove and discard the bay leaf and any unopened clams. Sprinkle with the cilantro and serve immediately.

PORTUGUESE SEAFOOD STEW *Cataplana* is the name of both this dish and the vessel used to cook it. A distinctive clam-shaped copper pot with side-mounted clamps to hold it closed during cooking, the cataplana originates from the Algarve region of southern Portugal. Looking like a flying saucer, it is of Moorish design and is most likely an ancestor to the modern steam cooker.

We have adapted this recipe to make it in a regular pot. If you would like to use a cataplana instead, cut the recipe in half (the vessel can hold only enough for two) and secure the lid once all of the ingredients are in the pot. Cook for 2 minutes before taking the cataplana to the table on a napkin-lined plate. Open the latches carefully, away from you, to let the steam escape.

Enjoy this delightful stew with crusty bread and a glass of Vinho Verde. • **SERVES 4 AS A MAIN COURSE**

Heat the oil over medium-high heat in a large pot. Add the shallots, garlic, and red pepper flakes. Cook for 1 minute. Add the clams, mussels, and squid and cook for 2 minutes. Add the tomato puree, white wine, broth, shrimp, cod, and lobster, if using. Season with salt and pepper to taste.

Cover the pot with a tight-fitting lid. Cook for 3 minutes.

To serve, ladle the seafood and broth into 4 warmed bowls.

3 tablespoons extra virgin olive oil

2 shallots, finely chopped

2 small garlic cloves, minced

$1/8$ teaspoon crushed red pepper flakes

1 pound clams, well scrubbed

1 pound mussels, well scrubbed

8 ounces cleaned squid, bodies cut into rings, with tentacles

1 cup tomato puree, preferably San Marzano

$2/3$ cup dry white wine

$1^{1}/2$ cups low-sodium chicken broth

8 ounces peeled and deveined medium shrimp

8 ounces skinless cod fillets, cut into 8 pieces

2 cooked lobster tails, split, shell on (optional)

Sea salt and freshly ground black pepper

THE SURPRISING WINES OF PORTUGAL

MANY PEOPLE THINK OF PORT AND MADEIRA as the only wines made in Portugal. Granted these wines are steeped in tradition and are readily available in wine shops and restaurants; however, Portugal should not be overlooked when searching for wines to drink with a meal.

The biggest problem with Portuguese table wines is probably public relations. Most of the words for the grape types and growing areas in Portugal are so foreign looking and sounding to American ears. Intrepid wine buyers will be rewarded, though, with terrific values in both dry white and red wines. Here are some tips for navigating the Portuguese wine section of your favorite wine store or internet source.

Several unusual-sounding white grapes are blended together to make most of the white wines in Portugal. Alvarinho is the most important white grape in a wine called Vinho Verde. The perfect summer white, Vinho Verde is light, spritzy, and low in alcohol. The best have lovely floral notes and subtle stone-fruit flavors. Even though Vinho Verde means "green wine," it refers to the fact that the wine is made to be drunk young. Look for producers Quinta da Aveleda, Quinta da Pedra, Paco de Teixeiro, and Palacio da Brejoeira.

Portuguese reds are where it gets interesting. These wines are rustic, full bodied, and distinctive. Most of the reds spend time in Portuguese or French oak, giving the wines a velvety smoothness.

The modern-day red wine revolution started in the Douro Valley in the late 1950s. A wine called Barca Velha, aged in Portuguese oak and made only in the best years, showed that Portugal could produce excellent, age-worthy still wines made from port grapes.

The best-known reds come from the Douro Valley and the Dão region, which is just to its south in north-central Portugal. Dão wines are made with Touriga Nacional, considered Portugal's finest grape. The wines are rich and well balanced.

The region of Bairrada is named for the rich clay soils of this Atlantic coastal plain. The Portuguese word *barro* means "clay." Baga is the predominant grape variety. Baga can be acidic but mellows with age, displaying grapy fruit and soft tannins. Other grapes grown in Bairrada are Tinta Pinheira, Castelão Frances, and Cabernet Sauvignon.

Alentejo covers most of southern Portugal, bordering Spain on the east. It is the country's biggest agricultural region, known for olives, cork trees, and grapes. The best wines are made with the Periquita grape. Vineyard yields are very low due to the sun-baked growing conditions, creating powerful, ripe wines of quality and character. These wines have lush, plummy fruit flavors and go well with grilled meat, roast pork, and goat cheese.

Also look for wines from Estremadura, a hilly area north of Lisbon. There are a few small estates growing Cabernet Sauvignon and Chardonnay, but Jose Nieve Correira, a champion of traditional grape varieties, produces noteworthy oak-kissed wines of rich berry fruit and graceful acidity.

When buying, look for the word *quinta*. These are private estates that produce and bottle their own wines. Here is where you'll find the best in quality and innovation. The word *garrafeira* on a label means that the wine has been aged in tanks or barrels for at least two years and at least one year in the bottle before release.

Our producer recommendations are Quinta dos Murças, Quinta de Saes, Quinta de Pelleda, Quinta do Carvalhinho, J.M. Fonseca, João Portugal Ramos, Luis Pato, Quinta de Pancas, and Quinto do Carmo, which is partially owned by Château Lafite-Rothschild.

ATHENS

THE FIRST WINE BAR

CONSIDERED THE BIRTHPLACE of Western civilization, Greece is also responsible for introducing wine to the rest of the world. Reintroduce yourself to some classic Greek dishes that are perfect for an easygoing grazing-styled menu. These simple make-ahead recipes are crowd pleasing and fun to serve with the modern wines of Greece.

Mediterranean Lemonade

Taramasalata with Salmon Caviar

Fava Bean Puree

Whipped Feta and Roasted Red Pepper Spread

Greek Pizza with Feta, Black Olives, and Oregano

Roasted Artichokes

Flaming Ouzo Shrimp

Oven-Roasted Greek Potatoes with Skordalia

Spicy Chicken Wings with Tzatziki Sauce

Grilled Marinated Lamb Chops with Giant White Beans

Grilled Marinated Greek-Style Pork Sandwiches

The Wines of Greece

MEDITERRANEAN LEMONADE Ouzo, the Greek anise-flavored liqueur, usually consumed straight up, is also terrific when made into a cocktail. Mixed with ouzo, honey, and fresh mint, lemonade takes on an exotic Mediterranean twist.

- **MAKES 1 COCKTAIL**

Combine the ouzo, lemon juice, simple syrup, honey, and mint leaves with some ice in a cocktail shaker. Strain over ice into a glass and garnish with fresh mint.

1½ ounces ouzo

1½ ounces fresh lemon juice

1 ounce Honey Simple Syrup (page 147)

½ teaspoon honey

5 fresh mint leaves, plus mint for garnish

TARAMASALATA WITH SALMON CAVIAR Two kinds of fish roe go into this rich, salty classic Greek spread: the dry salt-cured *tarama* and salmon caviar, which can be found in gourmet markets. You can prepare this recipe in advance and refrigerate it for several hours, even overnight, until needed. Serve with toasted pita wedges. • **MAKES 1½ cups**

1 pound white bread, preferably a day old

2½ tablespoons tarama roe

1 medium onion, grated

1½ tablespoons fresh lemon juice

Pinch of freshly ground white pepper

½ cup extra virgin olive oil, plus more for drizzling

1 ounce salmon caviar

Fresh chives, for garnish

Cut the crust from the bread and discard. Cut the soft white bread into large chunks and place in a large bowl. Add enough water to cover and soak until just soft, 15 to 20 minutes.

Squeeze the water out of the bread with your hands and transfer the bread to a food processor with the tarama, onion, lemon juice, and pepper. With the processor running, slowly drizzle in the oil. Once all of the oil has been added, blend until light and fluffy, about 1 minute.

Scrape into a bowl and garnish with the salmon caviar, a few snips of chives, and a drizzle of extra virgin olive oil.

FAVA BEAN PUREE
Serve this cool spread with hot-off-the-grill pita. See photograph on page 177. • **MAKES ABOUT 1½ cups**

Soak the fava beans overnight in cold water to cover by at least 3 inches.

Drain them, peel off the outer pale green shell of the favas, and put the beans in a medium saucepan. Add enough cold water to cover by 2 inches and bring to a boil over medium-high heat. Cook until tender, about 20 minutes. Drain and set aside to cool.

When the favas have cooled completely, puree them in a food processor with the garlic and olive oil until smooth and light, about 1 minute. Season with salt and pepper to taste. The puree can be covered and refrigerated overnight. Bring to room temperature before serving.

To serve, scoop the puree into a bowl, drizzle with olive oil, and top with capers and arugula.

1 cup dried fava beans

1 garlic clove

½ cup extra virgin olive oil, plus more for drizzling

Sea salt and freshly ground black pepper

1½ tablespoons capers, preferably salted, rinsed

5 arugula leaves, thinly sliced

WHIPPED FETA AND ROASTED RED PEPPER SPREAD
Easy to make, this spread has an enticing sweet and salty taste. See photograph on page 177. • **MAKES ABOUT 1 CUP**

Puree the roasted peppers with the cheese in a food processor. Add the olive oil and process until well combined. Season to taste with freshly ground pepper.

Scoop the spread into a bowl. This spread can be covered and refrigerated overnight. Bring to cool room temperature before serving.

2 roasted red bell peppers

8 ounces feta cheese

2 tablespoons extra virgin olive oil

Freshly ground black pepper

GREEK PIZZA WITH FETA, BLACK OLIVES, AND OREGANO
Here is a Greek-inspired pizza that is briny, sweet, tangy, and hard to resist. • **MAKES FOUR 12-INCH PIZZAS**

Extra virgin olive oil, for brushing

Pizza Dough (page 86) or
2 pounds store-bought
refrigerated pizza dough

12 ounces fresh mozzarella cheese,
cut into 1/2-inch pieces

4 beefsteak tomatoes, cut into
10 thin slices each

12 ounces feta cheese, crumbled

1 tablespoon plus 1 teaspoon dried
oregano

1 cup kalamata olives, pitted

Sea salt and freshly ground black
pepper

Preheat the oven to 500°F.

Have ready 2 nonstick cookie sheets or grease 2 regular cookie sheets with olive oil.

Working with one piece of dough at a time (cover the remaining dough with a moist kitchen towel until ready to use), flatten the dough on a floured work surface. Carefully stretch the dough out with your hands. Next, gently roll out the pizza dough into a 12-inch circle, about 1/8 inch thick.

Transfer the dough to a cookie sheet and brush with a thin layer of olive oil. Sprinkle one fourth of the mozzarella over the dough, spreading it to the edge. Then make a layer of tomato slices. Sprinkle with one fourth of the feta and top with 1 teaspoon of the oregano and one fourth of the olives. Season with salt and pepper. Repeat the process to make another pizza and bake both until golden brown, 12 to 15 minutes. Remove from the oven and repeat for the last two pizzas. Cut each pizza into 8 equal slices and serve immediately.

ROASTED ARTICHOKES These lemony, garlicky artichokes are so delicious yet easy to prepare. Baby artichokes are tender and easier to clean than large ones, since the choke is not fully developed. Dressed with a light vinaigrette, this dish can be served as an appetizer, or as an accompaniment to grilled steaks and chops. • **SERVES 4 AS AN APPETIZER OR SIDE DISH**

2 lemons

12 baby artichokes or 6 large

1 tablespoon chopped flat-leaf parsley leaves

1 teaspoon minced garlic

Pinch of crushed red pepper flakes

5 tablespoons extra virgin olive oil

Sea salt and freshly ground black pepper

Preheat the oven to 450°F.

Bring a large saucepan three-fourths full of water to a boil over high heat.

Meanwhile, grate the zest from one of the lemons and reserve 1 teaspoon in a small bowl. Juice the lemons and add 1 tablespoon juice to the zest; set aside. Reserve the remaining juice and the lemon shells.

Fill a large bowl with cold water and add 2 of the lemon halves and half of the remaining juice. Cut off all but 1 inch of the stem from each artichoke and then cut off the top fourth of each artichoke. Bend back and snap off the dark green outer leaves at the base until only the pale green and yellow leaves remain. Peel the stems with a vegetable peeler or paring knife to remove the coarse outer layer. If using baby artichokes, cut each artichoke in half lengthwise. If using large artichokes, cut into quarters. Using the point of a knife, remove any purple-tipped leaves or fuzzy choke from the center. Put the artichoke pieces in the cold lemon water.

Add the remaining 2 lemon halves and juice to the boiling water. Add the artichokes to the boiling water and cook for 1 minute. Drain and set aside.

For the dressing, add the parsley, garlic, red pepper flakes, and 3 tablespoons of the olive oil to the reserved lemon zest and juice mixture. Stir well to combine.

Heat the remaining 2 tablespoons of the olive oil in a large ovenproof sauté pan over high heat. Add the artichokes, season with salt and pepper, and cook for 1 minute. Transfer the pan to the oven and roast until the artichokes are tender and the edges are browned and crispy, 3 to 4 minutes.

Transfer the artichokes to a platter and drizzle with the dressing. Serve hot or at room temperature.

FLAMING OUZO SHRIMP This recipe is in the tradition of the flambéed Greek cheese dish known as *saganaki*. Ouzo is a Greek anise-flavored liqueur that matches well with shrimp.

Make sure that the ouzo goes on while the dish is very hot, or it will not light. And remember to stand back when flaming the shrimp. Serve with crusty bread to mop up the juices. ● **SERVES 6 AS AN APPETIZER OR 4 AS A MAIN COURSE**

Preheat the oven to 500°F.

Heat a large skillet in the oven for 5 minutes.

Remove the pan from the oven and add ¼ cup of the olive oil. Carefully layer the potato slices in the pan, slightly overlapping them. Top with the slices of jalapeño, garlic, and finally the shrimp. Season with salt and pepper. Drizzle with the remaining tablespoon of olive oil.

Return the pan to the oven and bake until the shrimp are opaque throughout, 5 to 7 minutes.

Remove the pan from the oven and add the ouzo. Stand back and carefully hold a lit match to the juices to flame the dish. As the flame begins to die down, squeeze the lemon over the shrimp. Serve immediately.

¼ cup plus 1 tablespoon extra virgin olive oil

1 russet potato, very thinly sliced

1 jalapeño pepper, thinly sliced

2 garlic cloves, thinly sliced

1¼ pounds peeled and deveined extra-large shrimp (under 15 per pound)

Sea salt and freshly ground black pepper

6 ounces ouzo

½ lemon

OVEN-ROASTED GREEK POTATOES WITH SKORDALIA

This recipe gives you Greek potatoes two ways. Yukon Gold potatoes are our favorite because they roast up crisp and buttery, and when tossed with herbs and red wine vinegar they are irresistibly good. The potatoes are then spooned onto garlicky *skordalia,* a potato almond dip, which catches all the juices. A grown-up version of chips and dip, these potatoes are great with roasted or grilled fish, steaks, and chops. • **SERVES 4 AS A SIDE DISH**

4 medium Yukon Gold potatoes, quartered

¼ cup plus 1 tablespoon extra virgin olive oil

2 tablespoons red wine vinegar

1 tablespoon chopped flat-leaf parsley leaves

1 teaspoon dried oregano

½ teaspoon sea salt

Skordalia (recipe follows)

Freshly ground black pepper

Put the potatoes in a medium saucepan and add enough cold water to cover by 2 inches. Bring to a boil over medium-high heat and cook until almost tender when pierced with a knife, 15 to 20 minutes. Transfer the potatoes to a colander to drain.

Preheat the oven to 475°F.

Heat ¼ cup of the olive oil in a medium ovenproof sauté pan over medium-high heat. Add the potatoes to the pan and toss to coat. Transfer the pan to the oven and cook the potatoes until crispy and golden brown, about 30 minutes, turning once halfway through cooking.

Meanwhile, make the vinaigrette in a bowl large enough to hold the potatoes. Whisk together the vinegar, parsley, oregano, and salt. Remove the potatoes from the oven and transfer to the bowl with the vinaigrette. Toss well to coat.

To serve, spread the skordalia on a serving platter. Top with the potatoes. Drizzle with the remaining tablespoon of olive oil and season with pepper. Serve immediately.

SKORDALIA This heady Greek garlic dip is deliciously addictive and also tastes great with grilled zucchini, fried fish, and marinated beets. Make the skordalia a day ahead and refrigerate.

MAKES 1½ CUPS

Put the potato in a medium saucepan and add enough cold water to cover by 2 inches. Bring to a boil over medium-high heat and cook until tender when pierced with a knife, 15 to 20 minutes. Drain and reserve the cooking liquid. Rice the potato while warm into a large bowl. Set aside to cool.

Puree the almonds, lemon juice, garlic, salt, pepper, and olive oil in a food processor until smooth, about 2 minutes. Stir the almond mixture into the potatoes, along with enough of the reserved cooking liquid to make a smooth and creamy mixture. The skordalia can be stored in an airtight container in the refrigerator for up to 3 days. Serve at room temperature.

1 medium russet potato, peeled and cut into 1-inch pieces

¾ cup sliced blanched almonds

3 tablespoons fresh lemon juice

2 large garlic cloves, peeled

¾ teaspoon sea salt

¼ teaspoon freshly ground pepper

2 tablespoons extra virgin olive oil

SPICY CHICKEN WINGS WITH TZATZIKI SAUCE This spice
blend gives these wings a truly unique taste. Not just spicy hot, they have layers of
flavor. Many who have tried these wings have developed a craving for them, making this
one of our most requested recipes. The creamy tzatziki sauce cools the fire. • **MAKES
ABOUT 24 WINGS**

1 tablespoon plus 1 teaspoon hot
   paprika

1 tablespoon ground cumin

1 tablespoon ground coriander

1 tablespoon ground caraway

1 teaspoon cayenne

1 tablespoon freshly ground black
   pepper

1 tablespoon sea salt

1/4 cup plus 2 tablespoons olive oil

2 garlic cloves, peeled

4 pounds chicken wings

Tzatziki Sauce (recipe follows)

Puree the paprika, cumin, coriander, caraway, cayenne, black pepper, salt, olive oil, and garlic in a blender or food processor until smooth to make a marinade.

With scissors, remove the inedible tips of the wings at the joint and discard. Put the wings in a shallow nonreactive dish. Pour the marinade over the wings and toss to coat evenly. Cover and marinate the wings in the refrigerator overnight or for up to 24 hours.

Prepare a charcoal grill, preheat a gas grill to medium-high, or preheat the oven to 375°F.

Grill the wings for 15 minutes, turn them over, cover the grill, and cook for another 15 minutes. Repeat this process, cooking the wings uncovered for 15 minutes, then covered for 15 minutes and turning them as before. After 1 hour of cooking time, the wings should be cooked through and crispy.

To bake the wings, lay the wings next to each other but not touching on a nonstick or foil-lined baking sheet and bake until crispy, about 45 minutes.

Serve the hot wings with the tzatziki sauce for dipping.

TZATZIKI SAUCE A refreshing component of the popular Greek gyros and souvlaki, tzatziki is the perfect condiment for these full-flavored wings and a great dip for vegetables too.

MAKES ABOUT 2 CUPS

Combine the cucumber and salt in a strainer over a bowl. Let drain for 20 minutes. Squeeze the cucumber with your hands to remove excess water. Transfer to a large bowl and add the yogurt, sour cream, olive oil, lemon juice, garlic, and mint. Mix well to combine. The tzatziki can be made in advance and refrigerated overnight. Serve chilled.

1/2 **long seedless cucumber, peeled and grated**

2 **tablespoons kosher salt**

3/4 **cup whole-milk yogurt**

1/2 **cup sour cream**

2 **tablespoons extra virgin olive oil**

1 **tablespoon fresh lemon juice**

2 **garlic cloves, minced**

2 **tablespoons finely chopped fresh mint leaves**

Freshly ground black pepper

GRILLED MARINATED LAMB CHOPS WITH GIANT WHITE

BEANS Marinating these lamb chops in red wine gives the meat a deep purple hue and spectacular flavor. • **SERVES 8 AS AN APPETIZER OR 4 AS A MAIN COURSE**

Season the chops with salt and pepper. Lay the chops flat next to one another in a nonreactive 13 x 9-inch baking dish. Sprinkle with the onion, garlic, lemon zest, lemon juice, rosemary, thyme, and bay leaf. Pour in the red wine. Turn the chops over, cover, and refrigerate for 2 hours, turning once halfway through.

To prepare the beans, place them in a medium saucepan and add enough water to cover by 2 inches. Bring to a boil over medium heat and cook until tender, 45 to 60 minutes.

Preheat the oven to 200°F.

Drain the beans and transfer to an 8-inch baking dish. Add the olive oil, garlic, rosemary, salt, and pepper. Cover and bake for 45 minutes.

Prepare a charcoal grill or preheat a gas grill to medium-high.

Remove the chops from the marinade and pat dry with paper towels. Season lightly with salt and pepper. Arrange on the grill and cook until nicely browned and grill marked, 3 to 4 minutes on each side for medium-rare, or until an instant-read thermometer registers 120°F when inserted into the thickest part.

To serve, divide the beans among warmed plates. Drizzle some of the garlic-rosemary-infused oil from the pan over the beans. Place the grilled chops on top of the plated beans. Serve immediately.

FOR THE LAMB CHOPS

1 rack of lamb, cut into 8 chops

Sea salt and freshly ground black pepper

1 small onion, thinly sliced

3 garlic cloves, minced

Grated zest of 1 lemon

2 tablespoons fresh lemon juice

1 tablespoon chopped fresh rosemary leaves

2 fresh thyme sprigs

1 bay leaf, crushed

$1^1/_2$ cups dry red wine

FOR THE WHITE BEANS

1 cup dried giant Peruvian white beans, soaked overnight

2 cups extra virgin olive oil

2 garlic cloves, smashed and peeled

2 fresh rosemary sprigs

$^3/_4$ teaspoon sea salt

$^3/_4$ teaspoon freshly ground black pepper

GRILLED MARINATED GREEK-STYLE PORK SANDWICHES

Here is our version of gyro, the well-known Greek specialty that is traditionally made with lamb and cooked on a long vertical skewer and sliced.

Readily available in grocery stores, pork butt is a tender and juicy cut of meat from the pork shoulder. After grilling the pork, slice it thinly and serve on pita with Tzatziki Sauce (page 189), fresh tomatoes, and chopped onions. It will make about 8 sandwiches.

- **SERVES 4 AS A MAIN COURSE**

5 garlic cloves, peeled

2 tablespoons whole-grain mustard

1/4 cup balsamic vinegar

2 tablespoons extra virgin olive oil

2 tablespoons dried oregano

1 tablespoon ground coriander

1 1/2 teaspoons grated lemon zest

1 teaspoon grated orange zest

1/3 cup fresh orange juice

1 tablespoon honey

1 teaspoon sea salt

1/2 teaspoon freshly ground black pepper

2 pounds boneless pork butt

Combine the garlic, mustard, vinegar, olive oil, oregano, coriander, lemon and orange zests, orange juice, honey, salt, and pepper in a food processor or blender.

Transfer the mixture to a resealable gallon-size plastic storage bag, add the pork, and seal the bag. Marinate overnight in the refrigerator.

Prepare a fire in a charcoal grill or preheat a gas grill to medium-high.

Remove the meat from the marinade, shaking off any excess, and place the meat on the grill. Close the cover and cook, turning the meat every 15 minutes, until an instant-read thermometer inserted into the thickest part registers 140°F, about 1 hour.

Remove the meat from the grill and let rest on a cutting board for 10 minutes. Slice the meat as thinly as possible and serve as described above.

THE WINES OF GREECE

IN ANCIENT TIMES, Greece played a fundamental role in the development of wine culture in Europe. More recently, Greece has experienced a growth of quality wine production with new generations of winemakers determined to show the world anew the potential of its native varietals.

Greek wines present an interesting challenge to wine drinkers. While the varied indigenous grape varieties are well established, many since ancient times, they are still comparatively unknown outside of Greece. Wines are named by growing regions, grape types, or proprietary name. Consumers need to become more familiar with the names of the wines, the regions, and the producers to recognize and enjoy these easy-to-drink, food-friendly wines. Then, with time and some sipping, you'll learn that Naoussa is made from Xynomavro grapes and is one of Greece's most important red varieties.

Although we mention only a few here, these wines are the most well-known Greek wines available in the United States.

Greece produces more white wines than red. Most are blends, and our favorites usually feature one of the following two grapes prominently: Assyrtico, often described as Greece's top white grape, makes crisp, dry wines that are excellent with seafood. When you visit the island of Santorini, this is the white wine you'll drink with your grilled octopus. Moscofilero is a pink-skinned grape that produces a white wine of elegant character, medium body, with subtle rose and floral aromas. It is a luscious cocktail wine that makes a smooth transition to the meal.

Greece's red wines have much to offer, from the easy-drinking, spicy wines made from Agiorgitiko grapes (also known as St. George), called Nemea, to the earthy, nutty, and juicy cherry fruit flavors of Naoussa. Some producers are blending Greece's indigenous grapes with Cabernet Sauvignon and Merlot with truly delicious results. Try Megas Oenos, a blend of St. George and Cabernet Sauvignon from Boutari, the historic family-run firm. These wines are not only delicious but terrific values as well and made with food in mind. Try any of these wines with the recipes in this chapter and you can't go wrong.

Look for wines from producers Boutari, Manousakis, and Skouras.

RESOURCE GUIDE

ACADEMIA BARILLA
Italian olive oils, cured meats,
balsamic vinegar, and cheeses
Bannockburn, Illinois
Phone: (866) 772-2233
www.academiabarilla.com

**BOTTEGA DEL VINO
CRYSTAL**
Purveyors of gorgeous Italian
hand-blown glassware
Chicago, Illinois
Phone: (312) 829-6750
www.bottegadelvinocrystal.com

BROWNE TRADING
High-quality seafood company,
family owned and operated
Portland, Maine
Phone: (800) 944-7848
www.brownetrading.com

THE CHEF'S GARDEN
Farmer Lee Jones grows the
finest vegetables, herbs, lettuces,
heirloom tomatoes, and more
Huron, Ohio
Phone: (800) 289-4644
www.chefs-garden.com

GUSTIAMO
Importers of authentic Italian
products of every kind directly
from artisan producers
Bronx, New York
Phone: (718) 860-2949
www.gustiamo.com

ISOLA IMPORTS
Cerignola olives and other Italian
imported products
Chicago, Illinois
Phone: (773) 342-2121
www.isolaimports.com

LA QUERCIA
American artisan cured meats
made from hormone-free pork
Norwalk, Iowa
Phone: (515) 981-1625
www.laquercia.us

MATERIAL POSSESSIONS
Artist-made dishes, glassware,
and tabletop and home decor
Chicago, Illinois
Phone: (888) 241-1190
www.materialpossessions.com

MEATS BY LINZ
Specialists in beef, veal, and
pork
Calumet City, Illinois
Phone: (708) 862-0830
www.meatsbylinz.com

MURRAY'S CHEESE
Phenomenal cheese shop now
offering gourmet products, gifts,
classes, and even a cheese blog
New York, New York
Phone: (212) 243-3289
www.murrayscheese.com

PASTURE 2 PLATE
Cured meats, sausages, fresh
game, wild boar, and mushrooms
Cicero, Illinois
Phone: (708) 652-3663
www.pasture2plate.com

PINN-OAK RIDGE FARMS
Fresh, free-range Wisconsin
lamb
Delavan, Wisconsin
Phone: (262) 728-9629
www.wisconsinlamb.com

PLITT SEAFOOD
Service-oriented, quality seafood
wholesaler to the best shops
and restaurants in the Midwest
Chicago, Illinois
Phone: (773) 276-2200
www.plittcompany.com

THE SPICE HOUSE
High-quality, wide-ranging
hand-selected spices,
including sumac
Chicago, Illinois
Phone: (312) 274-0378
www.thespicehouse.com

**TEKLA
INCORPORATED/LEONARD
SOLOMON'S WINES &
SPIRITS**
French, Spanish, Italian, Greek,
and Portuguese cheeses, wines,
chocolates, oils, vinegars, and
many of the pantry items in this
book
Chicago, Illinois
Phone: (312) 915-0466
www.winecheese.com

VIOLA IMPORTS
Organic rice and pasta, fresh
mozzarella, hand-crafted cheese
knives, and other Italian
specialty products
Elk Grove, Illinois
Phone: (847) 690-0790
www.violaimports.com

ACKNOWLEDGMENTS

Writing a cookbook involves many talented people, and we are pleased to recognize and thank the following participants for their contributions.

To our friend and photographer Jeff Kauck and his team, producer Janice Schultz, and prop stylist Andrea Kuhn, thank you for turning those snowy, February days into a sunny, Mediterranean dream, creating photos that made us hungry, using only natural light.

We are indebted to our agent, Michael Bourret at Dystel and Goderich Literary Management. Thank you for your continual support of our ideas and getting them to the right people.

To Rica Allannic, our editor, you asked all the right questions and listened to our answers. For your expertise and willingness to negotiate—"Okay, the tripe can stay, but the boar has to go"—our respect and gratitude.

Thanks to the production staff at Clarkson Potter, Christine Tanigawa and Joan Denman, and to Maggie Hinders in design for understanding the essence of our book and presenting our ideas so stylishly. To Christine Benton, *complimenti* for your careful and thoughtful copyediting.

To our dear friend Beth Partridge, many thanks for helping us refine these recipes. Your passion for cooking is astonishing. Without you, this book would not exist.

To Missy Robbins, thank you for your assistance with recipes and products and for your sense of what a great cookbook should be. For allowing us the time to work on this book while captaining the ship, we are eternally grateful.

As advocates for seeking out quality ingredients for any recipe, we thank our fervent, like-minded colleagues: Sofia Solomon of Tekla Incorporated; Beatrice Ughi from Gustiamo; and Alessandro and Stefano Bellini of Viola Imports. To all the farmers and purveyors who diligently supply great foodstuffs, we simply couldn't do it without you.

To Bob Hall for the beautiful glassware of Bottega del Vino in our photos. If the wine matters, absolutely, so does the glass.

Bravi to the talented Spiaggia and Mangia Trattoria staff Jason Goldsmith, David Gade, Efrain Medrano, Lupe Tiscareno, and Jose Burgos; you helped in so many ways. And to Steven Alexander for stopping by the shoot every day with wine on your way to the restaurant.

Carol Levy and Peggy Swartchild, thank you for the perfect tableware from Material Possessions for our food photography.

To our business partners and friends, Larry Levy and Todd Oldham, many thanks for setting an amazing stage at the Fairfax Hotel in South Beach for wine bar food at Enoteca Spiaggia.

To our friends who understand wine bar food, Janet Isabelli, Andy Hopper, Dan Pancake, and Les Pinsof; to the winemakers who have shared their wines and their philosophies; and to our restaurant guests who enjoy our food and wine pairings and come back for more, your enthusiasm is our motivation.

To our supportive families, the most critical and the most appreciative, we love you.

Tanti baci,
Cathy and Tony Mantuano

INDEX